lonely planet

PERFECT
DAY

D0775997

The Perfect Day
September 2006

Published by
Lonely Planet Publications Pty Ltd
ABN 36 005 607 983
90 Maribyrnong St, Footscray,
Victoria, 3011, Australia
www.lonelyplanet.com

Printed through The Bookmaker International Ltd. Printed in China

Cover Photograph Daniel New

Photographs Lonely Planet Images

ISBN 1741790506

Lonely Planet Offices
AUSTRALIA Locked Bag 1, Footscray,
Victoria, 3011
Phone 03 8379 8000 Fax 03 8379 8111
Email talk2us@lonelyplanet.com.au

USA 150 Linden St, Oakland, CA 94607
Phone 510 893 8555 Toll free 800 275 8555
Fax 510 893 8572
Email info@lonelyplanet.com

UK 72-82 Rosebery Ave London EC1R 4RW
Phone 020 7841 9000 Fax 020 7841 9001
Email go@lonelyplanet.co.uk

Publisher Roz Hopkins
Publishing Manager Chris Rennie
Commissioning Editor Ben Handicott
Publishing Planning Manager Jo Vraca
Creative Director Jane Pennells
Designer Mark Adams
Design Team Brendan Dempsey and Daniel New
Image Researcher Rachel Roche
Layout & Pre-Press Production Michael Ruff
Project Manager Annelies Mertens
Editorial & Production Manager Jenny Bilos
Editor David Andrew

With many thanks to
Simone Egger, Vanessa Battersby, Jennifer Garrett, Graham Imeson and Carol Chandler

CONTENTS

CITY HIGHLIGHTS
Emirates Palace | Counting the domes before dining under one of them.
Malls | Encountering the bizarre and the bazaar in one of the city's modern malls.
La Fana Restaurant | Taking a tour of the city from 19 floors up at Abu Dhabi's only revolving restaurant.
Water sports | Jet-skiing through the sunset at a hotel beach club.
City parks | Picnicking with the parrots in one of Abu Dhabi's many parks.

The Perfect Day in
ABU DHABI

A longstanding resident of Oman, **Jenny Walker** has visited every country in the Middle East.

The bartender apologised: as it was a holiday, the entertainment would be beginning early – at 23:30.

Indeed, it's hard to talk about a 'top day' in a city that specialises in 'top nights'. But then again, Abu Dhabi is also a city of top breakfasts, so it's worth a try. 'Rags to riches' is a phrase that occurs frequently in this wealthy, confident, capital city. My top day, however, would do some unravelling, starting in riches and undressing slowly from there. And it doesn't get much richer than the Emirates Palace: be-marbled, be-jewelled, be-domed and bedazzling, this is the place for be-reakfast. Slipping off the stilettos, I'll cross the breakwater for coffee in the Heritage Village and a glimpse of tonight's towers rising like organ pipes at the end of the corniche. Speaking of which, it's on with the trainers for a jog alongside the Gulf, flat-calm and reflective, just like the city after lunch. Umm, lunch? That would be into sandals, and up to La Fana, Le Royal Meridien's revolving restaurant, to anchor the city in sand-spits and slices of brilliant Middle Eastern sun. And for a bit of the sand and the sun it's a drive down Hamdan St in time to kick off shoes for sundowners on the Inter-Continental beach. Donning slippers and none too early, I'll taxi along Electra St, living up to its name in lights, for a demonstration of hat-popping condiments in the Japanese restaurant at the Beach Rotana. Next door to Abu Dhabi Mall for a promenade, local style, preferably cruising the 3rd-floor incense shops. And lastly, better be boots and no nippers for the nightly gold rush at 49'ers, opposite the mall. Well I say lastly, but let's keep a shwarma up the sleeve (if we're still wearing one), for the ritual pre-dawn picnic in one of the city's many parks. In fact, may as well enjoy a final descent from riches to rags and watch sunrise from a park bench.

The Perfect Day in
AUCKLAND

Sally O'Brien was raised in Seoul and Sydney and has been writing for Lonely Planet since 2001.

A good day in Auckland starts with a big breakfast and a truly great cup of coffee, so I head to Sheinkin on Lorne St for a fix.

Then I'm in the mood for souvenir shopping, and that means an authentic Flying Nun T-shirt from Little Brother on High St, followed by a perfect pair of trousers from Karen Walker. Now it's time to see a temporary exhibition at the New section of Auckland Art Gallery, with works by emerging and established contemporary local artists. And since you can't come to New Zealand without taking part in an extreme sport of some kind, I head to the Sky Tower to do the Sky Jump – a 192m descent. The adrenaline rush needs some food, so lunch at Soul on Viaduct Harbour is a must. The whitebait fritters (washed down with NZ Sauvignon Blanc) are the best in town and the atmosphere here is always buzzing. The maritime mood continues at the Maritime Museum, and then I head for an after-work (well, it's after work for everyone else) cocktail somewhere on Vulcan Lane – perhaps in the Gin Room. That night a group of us heads out for either a Japanese or Korean BBQ and a full roster of bar-hopping and rock 'n' roll gigs along the always entertaining K Rd. Plans are made to spend tomorrow on beautiful Waiheke Island, so it's a good thing I head home before the sun's up, unlike many of the other revellers along this nocturnal strip.

A freighter berthed alongside the Auckland city skyline. **Peter Bennetts**

HIGHLIGHTS
Beaches | Play, swim, laze, surf, sunbathe...

Seminyak nightlife | From restaurants to bars you won't be bored – or underfed.

Walking | Gorgeous river valleys and verdant rice paddies are just some of the highlights of the countryside near Ubud.

Balinese culture | Immerse yourself night and day in the local dance, art and music.

Doing nothing in Ubud | Even the cheapest accommodation has a restful vibe that'll have you kicking back with a good book in no time.

The Perfect Day in
BALI

Ryan Ver Berkmoes first visited Bali in 1993 and continues to be surprised and enthralled by it.

If I was staying in South Bali, I'd get up and go for a walk on the simply amazing beach that runs north almost from the airport in the south past Kuta, Legian and Seminyak, and onwards for at least another 5km (3.1mi).

This sweep of sand is buffeted by the kind of surf that first put Bali on the map for backpacking boarders in the 1960s. Rent a beach chair, join in a volleyball game with some locals, take surfing lessons, get a massage from one of the veteran masseuses or buy a beer from one of the many vendors – it's a pretty mellow scene that stretches as far as you can see. Furthermore, if you need to get from, say, Seminyak to Kuta fast, taking the beach route is the quickest and prettiest way to get there by far. At night I'd head to one of the myriad of superb restaurants in Seminyak for dinner, later hitting one of the many clubs of the moment. If I was staying in Ubud, I'd get a room with a view and simply chill out. I might stir once in a while to go for a walk through the rice fields and river valleys, but I'd soon find myself back by a pool. I would definitely make time to wander the streets and check out some of the cool little shops which seem to appear like mushrooms after the rain. At night – in fact, every night – I'd catch one of the entrancing dance performances offered at venues all over town.

After that I'd dine alfresco at one of the many fine local restaurants.

CITY HIGHLIGHTS

Musée National | Explore one of West Africa's finest museums, featuring wooden masks and colourful textiles.

Grand Marché | Jostle for elbow-room and lose yourself in the clamour of the mother of all Bamako markets.

Live music | Dance to the irresistible rhythms of Mali's world-famous musicians at any number of buzzing outdoor venues.

San Toro Restaurant | Dine amid African artwork and traditional architecture while a musician caresses the *kora*.

Musée Muso Kunda | Pay homage to Mali's women at this fine museum.

The Perfect Day in
BAMAKO

Africa entices **Anthony Ham**, contributor to *Africa on a Shoestring*, into a yearly extended visit.

Bamako days begin late – this is a city that loves to party by day and takes a while to get going in the morning.

So what better way to get the day started than with a Parisian-style pastry at Relax or the downtown Pâtisserie le Royaume des Gourmands. By the time I've gorged on coffee and croissants I'm ready for Bamako, where all the world's a market. The Grand Marché is enough to wake anyone up, but if it all gets too much, there's always the Musée National with its statuesque masks and stunning textiles. By now it's lunchtime so I'd find myself eating again, this time fine African food at the museum branch of African Grill. In need of more culture, I'd tour the Musée de Bamako and the Musée Muso Kunda. Marché N'Golonina has a more earthy and clamorous charm. But if I can't find that special handicraft I'm after there, I'd head out to the Hippodrome and to Mia Mali, possibly the most innovative and beautifully stocked boutique in the country. By late afternoon, I would be in search of that big African sunset, either with a few quiet drinks by the Niger River at the Mandé Hôtel or, if I'm feeling energetic, from the elevated vantage point of Point G. Dinner would definitely be at San Toro Restaurant, where the *kora* playing always makes me think of angels, and the great African food fortifies the stomach for yet another night of revelry. There are so many places in Bamako to hear Mali's wonderful musicians performing live that the choice can be an agonising one. If it's a Friday or Saturday, I can usually narrow it down to the gritty vibe of Le Hogon, the more attractive Éspace Bouna or among the sophisticates at the French Cultural Centre. Then again, it's as much a question of who's playing as the ambience. If Oumou Sangaré is playing at her Wassulu Hôtel or Salif Keita is packing his Moffou nightclub to the rafters, just you try and stop me getting in.

CITY HIGHLIGHTS

Chatuchak | Not just about shopping and eating, the Weekend Market offers a window into the diversity of Thai society and culture.

Wat Pho | A beautiful temple housing the tremendous reclining Buddha and a wonderful massage school.

Lumphini Park | A breath of fresh air, greenery and civic conviviality in the city centre.

Banglamphu | For the entertainment of the Khao San travellers' enclave and the funky cafés of Pra Athit.

River boats | Public ferries allow great sightseeing – jump out wherever you want to eat and explore.

The Perfect Day in
BANGKOK

The widely travelled **Annabel Hart** has contributed to a number of Lonely Planet titles.

Wake up in Bangkok and know that anything is possible.

I begin by walking the busy streets to select the best egg-noodle soup with wontons and red pork – a delicious, ubiquitous dish and an excellent hangover cure. A trip down the river is next, a wonderful breezy way to see the city and its monuments without choking to death. A stop at a riverside restaurant is always scenic and delicious; I'd probably seek out some soft-shelled crab with glass noodles at In Love restaurant at Thewet pier. Jumping off the ferry at Saphan Taksin, I would skytrain it up to Siam for some shopping, leaving time at the end of the day

for a calming swim, a Thai massage and a bag of mangosteens. Bangkok is all about alternating the pampering with the hard yards, the chic heights with the seething streets. An ideal evening, therefore, involves somewhere very fancy for drinks, like sunset at Vertigo (the rooftop bar at the Banyan Tree Hotel) and then local street food on plastic chairs in the warping heat. The car park on the corner of Ratchadamri Road and Soi Sarasin, near Lumphini Park, is great, as are many places in the Samsen sois in Banglamphu. Alternatively, I'd go for cold beer and salty beans at the little makeshift bars that line the Chatuchak weekend market (wonderful post-shopping ambience

as the market is closing) followed by an inner-city restaurant. Dinner cruises run by the fancy hotels are super-touristy but a great treat for visitors. If there's a night out on the cards I would start with G&Ts at Cheap Charlie's on Sukhumvit Soi 11 or Admakers (great live music) on Soi Lang Suan, and let the random and glorious energy of the city decide the rest. A midnight snack and a walk down the human zoo of Khao San Rd is always entertaining, especially when the bars close and the messy hordes spill into the street.

CITY HIGHLIGHTS

La Sagrada Familia | Marvel at Gaudí's most astonishing creation – curvaceous spires and exotic flourishes that could only emerge from the mind of a genius.

Parc Güell | Wander amid the zany curves of Gaudí's wonderful contribution to landscape architecture.

La Rambla | Soak up the essential Barcelona experience with some of the best street performers in the world.

Barri Gòtic | Lose yourself in one of the Mediterranean's liveliest and most labyrinthine old quarters.

Museu Picasso | Linger over the master's early works spread through five lovely mansions.

The Perfect Day in
BARCELONA

Inveterate traveller and writer **Anthony Ham** is also a resident of Madrid.

I'd be up early for a stroll along La Rambla, while the street performers and flower shops are still setting up and I can appreciate one of the world's most beautiful city walks.

By the time the crowds arrive, I'd be in Café de l'Opera, reading my newspapers and keeping an eye out for the latest zaniness to grip Barcelona. Then I'd hop on the Metro and track down the exuberance of Gaudí, whose childlike brilliance elevates Barcelona above all other Mediterranean cities.

His creations: La Sagrada Familia, Casa Batlló and Parc Güell never disappoint, no matter how many times I visit. By now it's lunchtime so I'd head for the outdoor tables of the Plaça Reial – a touch of Spain in this most cosmopolitan and European of cities. It's gritty, neoclassical and home to Gaudí's first tentative forays, in the form of lampposts. Picasso lived near here so I'd go for a culture fix at his museum, the Museu Picasso. En route I'd pause for another pit stop in the Plaça de Sant Josep Oriol, one

of the Barri Gòtic's prettiest squares. By late afternoon, I'm rejuvenating flagging energy levels with a sea breeze along Barcelona's beach. Maybe I'd have a siesta and maybe not, but I would never forsake a night out in El Born, one of the coolest *barrios* of Barcelona. Here the shops ooze style, the restaurants attract an offbeat crowd and the cosy little bars provide my favourite evening haunts. Depending on how long I stay, I wouldn't be up quite so early the next morning...

Chimney pots like medieval helmets line the roof of Antonio Gaudí's La Pedrera (Casa Mila). **Martin Hughes**

CITY HIGHLIGHTS
Roman baths | Visit the monumental remains of Bath's steaming soul.
Georgian architecture | Soak up the atmosphere while wandering the streets.
Bizarre Bath Walk | See the eccentric side of this ever-so-elegant city.
Walcot St | Discover boho Bath at its best, from stinky cheeses to vintage clothes and reclaimed fireplaces.
Museum of Costume | Strut through the history of fashionable dress since the 16th century at Bath's most prestigious address.

The Perfect Day in
BATH

Etain O'Carroll lives and works in Oxford and wrote for the *Britain* and *England* guidebooks.

Bath just oozes an air of 18th-century exclusivity. Nothing should be done quickly here.

I wake up slowly, soak up the atmosphere, slip gracefully out of that cast-iron bed and wander down through the honey-coloured streets to an elegant but secluded cafe for a languid breakfast. The best thing about Bath is just taking the time to appreciate the incredible streetscapes all over the city. I stroll for several hours, avoiding the crowds and Bath's most famous Georgian masterpieces, the Royal Crescent and the Circus, straying instead into the deserted side-streets where more humble buildings tell the real story behind this wonderful city. By then I've worked up an appetite and lunch is either a steady grazing in the Guildhall Market or a more hearty affair at the funky Adventure Cafe, a Bath institution. From here I pop into the Victoria Art Gallery for a look at the latest exhibition before wandering over to Walcot St to ramble through the reclamation yards, nibble on fine cheeses or find some vintage clothing. Feet and calves aching, it's time to slip back into modern life with some chilled drinks at Pulp or Raincheck, or, if the lineup grabs me, a show at the Theatre Royal or Rondo. Dinner with friends at the Walrus and Carpenter or Wife of Bath often flows into late-night drinks at the Common Room, a twirl on the dance floor at Moles, and a glorious stroll home through the gorgeous terraces and crescents of this World Heritage city.

The Perfect Day in
BEIJING

Robert Kelly lives in Taipei in Taiwan, off the coast of China, with his wife and two cats.

I've got to get out for a bike ride in the morning, not just to clear the cobwebs, but also to remind myself why I love this city.

There's always something charming or wondrous to catch your eye. It could be a park filled with t'ai chi practitioners, or row upon row of Qing dynasty courtyards that have withstood (or not) the test of time. After a few hours of riding I settle into a local shop for a dumpling-and-beer breakfast (it's Beijing!). Then I wander over to the Forbidden City. I won't go in today (it requires a morning and afternoon), but I will skirt the outside walls and soak in the atmosphere. After

passing through the Gate of Heavenly Peace I find myself in the underpass crossing over to Tiananmen Square. I always like to see what's being sold down here. Today, it's propaganda-era posters. Up in the square, I watch the touts flying immensely long kites and then halt before the Arrow Tower. I can't see this immense fortification without picturing myself up on the wall walk, freaking out as the Mongol hordes descend on the city. Still, the Mongols did bring lamb hotpot to Beijing, and I am so grateful for this that I'm going to have it for lunch. Afterwards I head to Liulichang St for some curio and *faux*-antique browsing. By the time I find

something I like, it's late in the afternoon, and there's no better time to head out to the Summer Palace. It may seem an odd time to go, especially considering how enormous the place is and how early it closes (18:00 in summer), but here's a secret: they don't kick you out right away after closing time. I stay to watch the sun set and finish off the experience with a beer down by the quiet shore of Kunming Lake. When I get back to the city I'm tired, but I agree to meet some friends for snacks and drinks on Lotus Lane. Just one beer, I say. Well, maybe two (it's Beijing!).

CITY HIGHLIGHTS

Corniche | Take part in a Beirut ritual with a leisurely afternoon stroll on the Corniche.

Sheesha | After a stroll, take a *sheesha* (water pipe) break at a café overlooking Pigeon Rocks.

Long lunch | Take a slow VIP-watching lunch at one of the downtown restaurants.

National Museum | Experience 6000 years of history in a couple of hours.

Nightlife | Follow Beirut's young and beautiful into one of Rue Monot's hot clubs or hit Gemmayzeh's Rue Gouraud for the bar-hopping scene.

The Perfect Day in
BEIRUT

Syria & Lebanon author **Terry Carter** claims he'd fly to Lebanon for dinner if flights were cheaper.

My day starts a little late due to the lure of Beirut's nightlife – but more of that later!

To cure the ills of the night before I usually leave the laptop at the hotel, skip the wifi-enabled cafés and head straight to Ristretto for excellent spicy eggs. Here I'll check out the Daily Star supplement in the International Herald Tribune to see if there are any exhibitions or performances worth taking in that night. If I have first-time visitors, we'll check out the small but beautifully renovated National Museum of Beirut, which took a pounding during the civil war. Back in the city centre, we'll visit the sombre memorial to assassinated former prime minister Rafiq Hariri next to Martyrs Square. Then we'll check out the progress of the excavations of Roman ruins adjacent to my favourite Italian eatery in Lebanon, La Posta, in the Downtown. We'll stop here for lunch unless my guests want to eat some excellent Lebanese food, in which case we'll head to the ever-popular Al Balad down the street. If it's good weather, we'll head to Bay Rock Café with its excellent view of Pigeon Rocks for some sunset *sheesha*. With the clubs of Rue Monot on the night's agenda, it's a good time for a quick nap before our dinner reservation at L'o on Rue Gouraud at 21:00. After a satisfying meal, we'll check out the buzzy little bars on the street such as Dragonfly or Torino Express, or for something quieter, wrangle a table at atmospheric Gemmayzeh Cafe for wonderful oud (Arabic lute) playing and soulful singing. By this time (about midnight) we're ready to check out the scene at Rue Monot, where the bars change with frightening frequency, but the vibe remains the same. If it's a really big night, then we'll head to the granddaddy of Beirut's clubbing scene, B018, with its brilliant décor and decadent vibe. By the time we're finished there, Ristretto will probably be opening.

CITY HIGHLIGHTS

Crown Liquor Saloon | Sink a pint or two in Belfast's most famous pub.

West Belfast | Take a guided walking tour to see the political murals and hear history from the locals' perspective.

City Hall | Join a free guided tour of the sumptuous civic building.

Lagan towpath | Stroll along the river and work up an appetite for a waterfront lunch.

Cave Hill | Hike to the city's highest point for panoramic views.

The Perfect Day in
BELFAST

A native of Ireland's wet 'n wild west, **Etain O'Carroll** wrote for the *Ireland* and *Britain* guides.

The first dilemma of a day in Belfast is whether to indulge in the artery-clogging Ulster Fry on offer or to save the soul and go for toast instead.

The fry usually wins and then that means hitting the streets with vigour to pacify a guilt-ridden, deadweight of a stomach. I generally head off in the direction of South Belfast to enjoy the leafy suburbs, classical University buildings and the hidden treasures of the Palm House and Tropical Ravine at the Botanic Gardens. If I'm feeling in need of a cultural fix I'll nip into the Ulster Museum for a quick browse before heading down Botanic Ave again for lunch at whatever new café or restaurant has sprouted

since my last visit. After lunch it's time to organise the best part of the day, a guided tour of West Belfast. No matter how many times I return I still find it fascinating and there's no better way to see it, and understand its history, than with a local. Belfast has changed so much in recent years it's hard to keep up, especially on the bar and restaurant scene. And in a city where you can hire former riot control vehicles for hens' nights you know there's going to be some good nightlife. So it's best to start early with a late afternoon pint in the Crown Liquor Saloon, Belfast's most elegant Victorian pub, before moving on to the traditional Morning Star

or John Hewitt Bar for the other half. With good food and live music it can be impossible to pull yourself away, so sometimes you just have to settle in for the night, particularly when the debate over which of the city's new gastro-pubs and trendy restaurants you should be eating in just keeps on going.

CITY HIGHLIGHTS

Reichstag | Stand in awe of the weighty history of this Berlin landmark, then head up to its famous glass dome for 360° city views.

Museumsinsel | Feast your eyes on treasures from around the world in this superb cluster of museums.

Schloss Charlottenburg | Revel in royal pomposity and stroll in the fabulous gardens.

Jewish Museum | Get ready for bold architecture and a journey through 2000 years of tumultuous Jewish history.

Potsdamer Platz | Sample the vibrant scenes and architecture of Berlin's newest city quarter.

The Perfect Day in
BERLIN

Berlin guide author **Andrea Schulte-Peevers** was born and raised in Germany.

Berlin moves to a different rhythm than other metropolises. Much of the city doesn't wake up until mid-morning and, if possible, neither do I.

Once the brain synapses begin firing, it's time to get the day going with that great Berlin tradition: a leisurely breakfast. I pick up a newspaper, then grab a table in the sun at Cafe Berio in Schöneberg. It's Saturday and the city's best farmers market on Winterfeldtplatz is in full swing. I sip a latte, munch my croissant and watch the world on parade: young dads carrying their kid in a sling, bleary-eyed hipsters just returning from a night on the town, hunched grannies lugging their shopping bags. I've got my mind on a different market, so I hop on the U-Bahn and head north to the Mauerpark and its big flea market. As I ferret for treasure my mobile bleeps with a text message from my friend asking me to join her in checking out the New National Gallery. Sounds good to me. After our culture fix, we gossip while strolling around the Tiergarten – its greenery redolent with the sweet smell of springtime – then decide to watch the sunset from the landmark dome atop the Reichstag. By now our stomachs are starting to rumble. We decide to go exotic and head over to Kasbah in Mitte to feast on our favourite Middle Eastern dish: *tajiine*, a fragrant stew of veggies, meat and a secret melange of spices. Later, we hook up with friends at Heinz Minki, a gorgeous beer garden right on the Spree River in Kreuzberg. A few more drinks alfresco at Anhalt, a glam bar next to a decidedly unglam gas station, and at Freischimmer with its casual vibe. Then we're off to nearby Watergate, still one of Berlin's most sizzling clubs. A few hours later, ears ringing, we quietly watch the sun rise over the river. Time to go home.

CITY HIGHLIGHTS

Sun soak | Catch rays and waves on the untamed beaches of Isla Bastimientos.

Night vision | Hike through the jungle of Isla Cristóbal – at night.

Explore a reef | Snorkel the protected reefs around·Cayos Zapatillas.

Wander the water | Explore miles of mangroves on an early morning kayak paddle around the islands.

Wind down | Bar hop in Bocas town – the archetypal Gringo Trail pit stop.

The Perfect Day in
BOCAS DEL TORO

Conner Gorry spent a year camping, backpacking and chicken bussing around Central America.

After three days, my supplications for sun finally pay off and I wake to rays pouring into my *cabaña* at La Loma Jungle Lodge.

From bed I watch a pair of monkeys rattling through the branches in the middle distance and weigh my adventure options: a six-hour jungle hike which promises wildlife and a long, savage beach at the end where I can body surf away my sore muscles; or a mellow *cayuco* (local canoe) paddle around the mangroves, followed by some snorkelling and exploring around Cayos Zapatillas (still a natural wonderland, despite its repeated use in the *Survivor* series). My sloth friend is still up the same tree where

I spied him yesterday, I notice, as I descend the hillside through the forest to breakfast on home-baked bread and local tropical fruit – some of which I've never seen before. Scheming over coffee, I decide the jungle hike will be way muddy after three days of solid rain and that snorkelling will be pointless too: the water will be too churned up and the visibility cruddy. A couple of the other guests second our hosts' suggestion: a trip to a seriously off-the-beaten track beach in the autonomous indigenous region of the Ngobe. But first, the mangroves: I head down to the dock and try and get in the *cayuco*. Instead, I'm in the water,

not once, but twice. On the third try I get it and I'm paddling off towards the two kids laughing at me while they fish for *ronco*. They're Ngobe I learn and are gathering lunch and dinner for their family of four. I watch and listen to a flock of green parrots frolicking in the trees before I'm pulled back by the intrigue of our beach trip and the possibility of staying overnight to see the leatherback turtles nesting.

A boat moored in shallow water next to a palm-lined beach. **Alfredo Maiquez**

CITY HIGHLIGHTS

Montserrate | Take a funicular ride up this Andes foothill with mammoth views of Bogotá.

Museo Botero | Enjoy this quirky collection of the Colombian artist's favourite sculptures and paintings.

Tejo | The traditional Colombian game of throwing a metal disc to burst a *mecha* (triangular envelope full of gunpowder). You'll need a local to take you.

Coffee, amigo | Sometimes served weak, but – when done right – it's as fresh as a bus ride over the mountains.

Zipaquira Cathedral | Dug out of a salt mine 31km (19 miles) north of town, this cathedral is spookily illuminated by blue lights.

The Perfect Day in
BOGOTÁ

Latin America habitué **Robert Reid** believes the region is best seen with a beard or eye patch.

Me, well, I like to stay in Bogotá's historic centre, La Candelaria, in the company of colonial-era cobbled streets and tight sidewalks that lead in all directions from the central Plaza de Bolivar.

But first I'd start with breakfast at a restaurant atop the Montserrate mountain, reached by a five-minute funicular trip a couple of kilometres north, and eat my eggs with full views of the sprawling capital. Then I'd taxi back to La Candelaria, and stop in the free and wonderful Museo Botero, highlighting the Colombian artist's revelry in all things fat, like fat snoozing presidents, fat women bathing, fat cats, fat fingers, fat birds.

A shop for Juan Valdez – the moustached coffee icon of Colombia – has a café out front, which is good for a quick espresso. For a long, late-afternoon lunch, Fulanitos is an excellent four-century-old restaurant decorated with old bullfight posters and specialising in food from the area around Cali – I'd take a sour *lulada* fruit drink with my plate of fish or chicken and look over terracotta rooftops. I might roam a few more backstreets, perhaps poke into an old cathedral or two, then check back at my base at the Platypus hostel/guesthouse to see what fellow travellers, or long-term NGO residents, are doing for the night – and bum a spot in a walking bar-hop around the district.

CITY HIGHLIGHTS

Beacon Hill | Take a walking tour of this classic Brahmin neighbourhood, complete with cobblestones and gas lanterns.

Freedom Trail | Follow the redbrick pathway to Boston's major colonial sights.

Charles River | Rollerblade along the Esplanade on a sunny afternoon.

Fenway Park | Take yourself out to the ballpark and watch the Red Sox hammer away at the Green Monster.

Mapparium | Listen to a pin drop within this stained-glass globe at the Christian Science Center.

The Perfect Day in
BOSTON

Kim Grant lives with her partner in a circa-1900 Victorian home in Dorchester, Boston.

Lace up the walking shoes; any good day in Boston begins and/or ends with walking around her intimate neighbourhoods.

Head to an outdoor café on Newbury St, where a stiff espresso will jolt you into checking out Boston's most fashionable offerings. There's plenty of eye candy decorating the shop windows and walking the streets. Stroll through the Public Garden and Boston Common on your way to meandering around Brahmin Beacon Hill, which is thick with cobblestone streets and gas lanterns. Find the alleyway where slaves used to seek haven from slavecatchers. Have lunch on Charles St before following the red

brick path known as the Freedom Trail. It may sound corny and touristy, but hey, you're in Boston. The seeds of America's revolution were sown here. Pop into a few sites that pique your interest like Paul Revere's House and the Old North Church. And most definitely, pop into the tiny mom-and-pop specialty food shops that have been here for decades. Fortify yourself with another espresso (and a ricotta *cannoli*) on Hanover St and chill out by watching sail boats from the Christopher Columbus Waterfront Park. Is it time for a drink yet? Faneuil Hall Marketplace has more than a few bars from which to choose. If you're lucky enough to get Red Sox

tickets, take the T over to the famed Fenway Park and root, root, root for the home team. A hot dog should hit the spot for sustenance, as will the dance clubs on Lansdowne St afterwards.

The Perfect Day in
BRIGHTON

After travel in over three dozen countries, **Korina Miller** set up home in southern England.

I start my day with an early morning wander through the lush, peaceful Queen's Park.

I make my way down St James's St, past early-morning shoppers and revellers still revelling from the night before, and join the regulars at the fantastic Red Roaster café in being grateful that decent coffee and fresh baking have become a common breakfast alternative in England to the more traditional murky cup of tea and fried everything. I then take in some retail therapy in the North Laines' boutiques, where everything comes designer-style – be it party frocks, tailored suits, kitchen aprons or herbal toiletries. I stop for lunch at Sejuice, where they whip up fabulous organic smoothies and do a mean peppermint *chai* latte. If the weather is on my side I get lunch to go and lounge in the Pavilion Gardens. Then it's down to the seafront for a long stroll towards Hove. I walk along the pounding surf, past the ghostly West Pier to my favourite Brighton monument, the serene Peace Statue. Once there I turn around and head east along the footpath, checking out the arty shops, galleries and kiosks housed in the waterfront arches. When I reach the Palace Pier I can't resist a ride on the surprisingly fast scream-inducing roller coaster. I then continue a little further east along the beach to where the crowds thin out, and take a dip in the always-icy sea. After that it's home to get glammed up for a night out, dinner at one of my favourite restaurants like Nou-Nou or Krakatoa, and then dancing at the Funky Buddha Lounge until the wee hours. It's all topped off with a nice cuppa at the reliably rowdy all-night Market Diner, where I can mix with other blurry-eyed locals but don't think I'll ever be quite English enough to stomach that breakfast fry-up – even at 04:00.

The Perfect Day in
BRISBANE

Gemma Pitcher is the author of the Lonely Planet guides to *Austria* and *Madagascar & Comoros*.

My favourite place to start a Brisbane Saturday is Fatboy's Cafe in Fortitude Valley, which serves up enormous piles of eggs and bacon for those who feel the need to soak up Friday night's overdose of cocktails.

Suitably fortified, it's time to browse the nearby Brunswick St markets in search of the perfect vintage handbag or an offbeat piece of artwork. Then I whistle up some Brisbane mates (plus their kids) and jump on the City Cat at Riverside, whizzing past the Botanic Gardens and under the Captain Cook Bridge to the Streets Beach on South Bank, Brisbane's answer to a true-blue surf beach (minus the waves, unfortunately). We sip super smoothies, munch hot dogs and sun ourselves on the imported sand before taking a dip in the pool and clambering over the climbing gyms. Tired but happy children head home while I get changed for a more grown-up night out – a meal overlooking the river at elegant Circa restaurant on Adelaide St. After that we take a stroll back up to the Valley for cocktails (Friday night is by now just a distant memory) at Sunbar Restaurant & Lounge, followed by some very silly dancing amid the 70s decor at Fringe Bar.

CITY HIGHLIGHTS

Lone Pine Sanctuary | Cuddle up to a koala for maximum photogenic cuteness.
Botanic Gardens | Watch frisking possums at night while strolling the Mangrove Boardwalk.
Mt Coot-tha | Admire the view of the whole city from the top.
Queen St Mall | Shop in the Mall's upmarket emporia.
Streets Beach | Sunbathe and swim at South Bank, complete with traditional Aussie lifeguards.

The CBD's busy modern skyline lines the snaking Brisbane River. **Juliet Coombe**

CITY HIGHLIGHTS

Grand Place | Be spellbound by Brussels' magnificent main square.

Place du Grand Sablon | Fossick for rare finds in weekend markets before melting over the nearby chocolatiers' boutiques.

Centre Belge de la Bande Dessinée | Get reacquainted with local lad Tintin and his mates.

Musées Royaux des Beaux-Arts | Revel in the Art-Nouveau architecture as well as the artistic treasures.

Parc de Bruxelles | Feel the serenity.

The Perfect Day in
BRUSSELS

Catherine Le Nevez lists Brussels as a favourite destination for its multilingual, multinational vibe.

Brussels' beating heart is the dazzling Grand Place, ringed by gilded buildings. It's the centre of a web of enticing narrow cobblestone laneways winding in myriad directions, all begging to be explored, so ambling the back streets checking out the bold comic-strip murals splashed on unsuspecting facades can easily absorb several hours.

Though winter's warmed by cosy open fires and steaming hot chocolate, any top day in Brussels is ideally in summer, when bouquets of brightly coloured café umbrellas brim onto the city's pavements – great for sitting back and listening to the clamour of the dozens of languages spoken throughout this multinational European hub. Those umbrellas come in handy for Brussels' inevitable sudden downpours – no one said the weather in Belgium was good, but hey, with beer, waffles and chocolate nonpareil, who's complaining? Browsing the shops and outdoor markets provides the perfect opportunity to explore hidden corners of the city. On weekends the Sablon antique quarter teems with treasure-hunters trawling the traders' open-air stalls. Any day of the week the flea markets at Place du Jeu-de-Balle overflow with a crazy mishmash of bric-a-brac and racks of cool vintage clothes. Window shopping the avant-garde fashions on Rue Antoine Dansaert, stopping for an engine-revving coffee and an ice-cold Jupiler beer at Walvis café, and lingering along Ave Louise to peek at the designer boutiques soak up what's left of the day. The gleaming EU quarter's the ultimate fix for political junkies, and cultural pleasures are on tap at the Musée des Instruments de Musique and the Musées Royaux des Beaux-Arts (Royal Museums of Fine Arts). At night, Rue St Boniface comes alive with buzzing restaurants and cafés – it's conveniently close to the bars of the St Gilles district as the sun's glow fades over Belgium's – and Europe's – cosmopolitan capital.

Watching the passing parade while having a drink at St Goriks square on a summer evening. **Joost de Bock**

CITY HIGHLIGHTS

The Danube | In it (from Margaret Island), on it (from Vigadó tér) or above it (from Castle or Gellért Hill), it's Budapest's blue ribbon.

Art-Nouveau architecture | Sinuous curves, stars, moons and suns – and no, you're not on drugs.

Thermal baths | Soaking *à la turque*, in a cathedral or while playing chess.

Music, music, music | It's everywhere, at the Liszt Music Academy, at the State Opera House, at the Sziget rock festival.

Statue Park | Monumental socialist mistakes on the trash heap of history.

The Perfect Day in
BUDAPEST

Journalist, former bookseller and *Budapest* author **Steve Fallon** lived in the city for several years.

Let's just say for the sake of argument that I wake up late on my last day in Budapest, work accomplished and conscience (if not head) clear.

I skip breakfast and head for the Gellért Baths; some things are best done on an empty stomach. After a therapeutic soak and a 15-minute tussle with a mountainous masseur, I hobble across Independence Bridge, glancing up behind me at my best girlfriend, the one holding the palm frond atop Gellért Hill, and jump on tram No 2, which runs along the river to Újlipótváros, Budapest's Upper East Side. There's no better place in town than the Móri Vendégl for some Hungarian soul food. From here it's just a hop, skip and a jump to Margaret Island. I may stroll, I may cycle, I may kip in the sun... But I'm doing it on the beaten track. In this city of passion and pricey real estate, lovers seize every opportunity and, frankly, any bush will do. Walking past Parliament it seems a shame to pass up the chance for another look at the Ethnography Museum – I just can't get enough of those hammers and sickles – but I need a fix of Art-Nouveau/ Secessionist architecture and the No 1 metro (the 'little underground') beckons. Sinuous curves, asymmetrical forms and other bizarre shapes now under my belt, I'm free to think about the really serious things – a slice of something sweet at Lukács coffee house or a sundowner at one of the terrace café-bars on Liszt Ferenc tér while eavesdropping on some diva doing her scales at the nearby Liszt Music Academy. Dinner will be at the Múzeum next to the National Museum, still my favourite upmarket Hungarian eatery after all these years (since 1885 to be precise). The rest of the evening will be debauched at one of the *kertek* – the 'gardens' (or any open space) open at night in the warmer months.

The Perfect Day in
CABO SAN LUCAS

An author of the *Mexico* guide, **Ray Bartlett** has wandered the globe for over a decade and a half.

If I've done Cabo right, I start with freshly squeezed orange juice, coffee, and a giant plate of peach-and-walnut waffles at my favourite B&B.

After the coffee kicks in, I head out to the beach to watch pelicans swoop around as the azure waters lap against Land's End. The key thing is to not have a plan. If you're planning it all out, you're already missing what Cabo's all about. Put down the watch, throw away the calendar, and just have some fun: I might have the *panga* (small motorboat) drop me off at Lover's Beach; I might stroll around the marina and see what's happening; or I might sit under a palm tree with my camera and

a good book and people-watch. Even if nothing happens, I'm still having a great time. Taking a good photo of the Arch has still eluded me, so I'll probably plot my next photo attack and hope to get pics that do it justice. To me, the Arch is Cabo...I want to get it right. Spectacular salt-rimmed margaritas get me through the afternoon's languorous heat. I'll find a shady spot and sip something as I scoff down a *chile relleno* or a fresh fish taco. If it's still hot I'll catch up on news and email at an Internet café, and then get into the water. It might be surfing, it might be snorkelling, it might just be floating around in a glass-bottomed *panga* looking at tropical

fish after a quick dip or two...but I've got to get wet or the day isn't right. At night I either mellow out to mariachi music and sip a glass of red in my favourite restaurant, or I head to the clubs and people-watch as the conga lines weave by. Sometimes I'll hit Cabo Wabo cantina in hopes of playing a game of pool with Sammy Hagar, or laugh at the Squid Row craziness if I'm in the mood. If I'm lucky, I'm asleep at about 03:00.

Rocky hills form a backdrop to Cabo's harbour. **Witold Skrypczak**

CITY HIGHLIGHTS

Egyptian Museum | Muddled but endlessly fascinating old museum full of mummies and bizarre antiquities.

Islamic Cairo | Sure there are many wonderful mosques here, but take time to explore the atmospheric streets too.

Citadel | Noteworthy mosques and museums, and the views of Cairo are brilliant.

City of the Dead | Gawk at the homes of Egyptians who live among the intriguing tombs and mausoleums.

Feluccas on the Nile | Take a ride or just sit back and watch them sail by in the sublime sunset over the Nile from the Semiramis lobby bar.

The Perfect Day in
CAIRO

Terry Carter has travelled extensively through the Middle East, where he was based until recently.

Once I've dragged myself out of my heavenly bed in Talisman, the deliciously Oriental hotel in the Downtown area, I'll hit one of the local stands for a fresh mango juice before snapping some photos in the atmospheric streets of Islamic Cairo.

Although the Khan Al-Khalili bazaar is worth a look (and tea and *sheesha* at Fishawi's Coffeehouse is obligatory), I prefer to avoid the touts and tacky souvenirs and indulge my love of the oud (Arabic lute) by visiting one of the finest craftsmen working today, Maurice Shehata (80 Sharia Masr we El Sudan, Hadayek El Kobba), and watch the guys there hand-craft musical instruments.

If I impulsively bought one, I'd better visit Nomad Gallery (14 Saraya Al-Gezira St, Zamalek) to pick up some colourful tribal textiles or Bedouin jewellery for my wife, and then check out Divan for excellent Egyptian music, books and DVDs. Back in the Downtown area, I have lunch in the amusingly kitsch-cool Felfela, before an afternoon of exploring the musty Egyptian Museum. No matter how many times you visit you'll always find some fascinating treasure on the dusty shelves that you missed the last time. If I want to see the Giza pyramids hassle-free, I head to the Oriental cool of El Sultan Lounge bar at the Oberoi Mena House to

watch the afternoon sun turn the pyramids pink while I sip on a cocktail. Otherwise, I head to my other favourite sunset spot at the Semiramis Intercontinental lobby bar where I can watch the *feluccas* sail on the Nile. A visit to Cairo is not complete without catching the mesmerising whirling dervishes at the Citadel, then taking a late dinner at the exotic Abu As-Sid restaurant, Zamalek, followed by drinks at the nearby funky La Bodega bar. If everyone's up for it, I'll make a call to see if Dina, Cairo's best bellydancer, is gracing us with her presence at the Semiramis. If she's dancing, it's going to be a long night...

CITY HIGHLIGHTS

Table Mountain | Panoramic views in every direction from the top.

Long St | Quirky boutiques, bars and restaurants.

Robben Island | Moving political insights.

Constantia | Vineyards, wine and whitewashed houses.

Townships | Jazz maestros, shebeen queens and pavement aristocrats in the townships.

The Perfect Day in
CAPE TOWN

Former safari consultant **Gemma Pitcher** wrote for the *South Africa, Lesotho & Swaziland* guide.

The first thing I do when I wake up in my flat in Rondebosch is to take a walk out onto the terrace and say good morning to the mountain.

If it's a clear day, the towering grey-blue bulk in front of me seems to be beckoning, and it's on with the hiking boots and off to walk to the summit. A few hours later, tired but elated, I sun myself on the rocks and admire the view before taking the cable car down again for a late breakfast at Lola's on Long St (where the lattes are to die for). To pamper my aching muscles, I head to the Long St Baths for a long session of steam bath, massage and sauna before a bit of leisurely retail therapy at my favourite quirky boutiques. I'll spend an hour or two lost in thought among the Africana of Clarke's bookshop, then try on ridiculous party dresses and scrabble for retro handbags at Second Time Around or Never on a Sunday. My credit card suitably swiped out, I scoff a curry roti and an ice-cream cocktail at Mojito's before grabbing my towel and hitting the beach (Camps Bay or Clifton if I'm feeling brave enough to compare my bikini – and my butt – with the beautiful people surrounding me!). If the southeasterly's blowing, I'll turn my back on the beach and instead head up to Constantia for a glass or two of sublime Pinot Noir among the rows of vines that nestle against the foot of the mountain. Sundrenched and satisfied, I'll meet friends for sunset cocktails at La Med in Camps Bay, then head back into town for an arthouse movie at the Labia cinema on Kloof St followed by my favourite butternut ravioli on the terrace at Green's. If I'm feeling frisky, I'll grab some friends and head down Long St for drinks and red hot gossip – maybe packed in with the throng at Jo'burg, star-spotting at Planet or lounging on the Versace sofa in the fabulously decadent M Bar.

CITY HIGHLIGHTS

Wat U Mong | Taste serenity in the temple's brick-lined meditation tunnels.

Soi Ban Haw | Slurp *khâo sawy* (curry noodles) in one of the Yunnanese Muslim restaurants.

Old City | Follow the winding cobblestone lanes to discover Thai cooking schools, crumbling stupas and semi-hidden bars.

Traditional massage | Get pummelled at one of the many massage centres.

Sunday Walking St | Browse Chiang Mai's best handicrafts, locally produced CDs and street food.

The Perfect Day in
CHIANG MAI

Legendary travel writer **Joe Cummings** has been author of the *Thailand* guide for over 20 years.

I start the morning with a steaming mug of locally roasted arabica and a plate of French toast at the Libernard Café.

After reading yesterday's Bangkok Post and watching local monks shuffle by on their morning alms rounds, I'll pedal my bike across the street as mist rises off the 150-year-old moats surrounding the old city. Once past the restored brick remnants of Pratu Tha Phae, I head for the geographic and cultural heart of Chiang Mai. First I stop at the Three Kings Monument to pay my respects to the founding fathers of Chiang Mai's Lanna kingdom. Afterwards I bike into the compound of the 1924-vintage provincial hall, a masterpiece of post-colonial Thai architecture now serving as a space dedicated to northern Thai art and culture, to check the latest exhibits. If I'm in the mood to contemplate more fine architecture, I'll head for one of the 33 historic Buddhist temples inside the old city quadrangle. The side-by-side Wat Chedi Luang, home to the tallest stupa (conical Buddhist monument) in Chiang Mai, and Wat Phan Tao, assembled from exquisitely carved wooden panels taken from a Thai palace, never fail to inspire. Then, I'll stop in at either Si Phen or Heuan Phen for a lunch of Chiang Mai sausages and flaming green chilli dip. Fuelled for further city explorations, I'll scoot through the narrow, winding *soi* (lanes) at random, ever marvelling at Chiang Mai street life, the noodle vendors, laughing schoolchildren, European backpackers searching for a guesthouse and young housewives hanging out their laundry. As the late afternoon traffic and heat get to be a bit much, I'll pack the bike into the back of a red *sawngthaew* (pick-up truck taxi) and ask the driver to head for the lower slopes of Doi Suthep, just west of the city. At the Huay Kaew Restaurant I'll enjoy a cold Singha while watching a waterfall tumble over tree-shaded rocks.

CITY HIGHLIGHTS

Wrigley Field | Catch a baseball game at the Cubs' iconic, ivy-walled home.

John Hancock Center | Look out over the sparkling city from one of the world's tallest buildings.

Millennium Park | Explore 'The Bean' sculpture and video-projecting fountains at downtown's green space.

Chinatown | Stock up on salted peach bits, jasmine tea and Hello Kitty coin purses after eating dim sum.

Devon Ave | Graze on samosas, kosher donuts and other global eats at Chicago's 'International Marketplace'.

The Perfect Day in

CHICAGO

Karla Zimmerman has been testing bar stools and cheering on the Cubs in Chicago for 16 years.

I start the day in Chinatown, wandering from bakery to bakery while nibbling a coffee-cream roll, chestnut cake and almond cookie in rapid succession, then shopping for staples like toast-scented Hello Kitty erasers and baseball-bat-shaped chopstick holders.

I get on the Red Line train and alight downtown near avant-garde Millennium Park, stopping for a long time to admire 'The Bean' sculpture and to watch it reflect the city skyline. I follow up with a visit across the street to the Chicago Cultural Center to gawk at the gorgeous interior and hear a free lunchtime concert. Next, I hop back on the Red Line and head due north

to Wrigley Field to catch a Cubs game. If the sun is shining and the breeze is blowing, there's nowhere in the city that beats an afternoon spent here; if the sun is obscured and the breeze blizzard-like, that sucks but at least tickets are easier to come by. I order a hot dog and Old Style beer and sigh as the Cubs get clobbered. Nothing heals the soul quite like ice cream, so it's off to Bucktown and Margies, an old-fashioned parlor that makes its own chocolates and hot fudge on the premises. I dawdle for a few hours around the little shops selling stylish clothing, oddball accessories, records and books in the

Bucktown/Wicker Park neighbourhood, then consider where to go for the evening's live music finale. Two venues nearby offer bands just about nightly: Phyllis', a former Polish polka bar that now hosts scrappy up-and-coming bands, and the Hideout, hosting indie-oriented rock, folk and country musicians. I stop in for a set at the former, finish with a nightcap at the latter, then cab it home, convinced once again that Chicago is my kind of town.

CITY HIGHLIGHTS

Blarney Castle | Bend over backwards to kiss the Blarney Stone (it's said Corkonians aren't allowed, to avoid a double-helping of the 'gift of the gab').

Bells of Shandon | Climb the bell tower to ring the city's famous bells.

Cork Arts Theatre | Catch an experimental theatre production.

Ó Conaill Chocolatiers | Treat yourself to exquisite hot chocolate at this family-run café and purveyor of handmade chocolates.

Sin É | If you're going to visit just one pub for traditional Irish music, this is the place.

The Perfect Day in
CORK

Catherine Le Nevez has travelled at every opportunity since her wanderlust kicked in at age four.

Home to the Republic's second largest population, Cork (Corcaigh) is cosmopolitan, cultural and compact – making it easy to jam-pack your days and nights.

For a hearty start, the Farmgate Restaurant – on the mezzanine of the English market with views down over the bustling stalls – is a perfect prelude to trawling more markets at the historic Coal Quay. Bargain to your heart's content for organic fruit and vegetables, home-baked goods, musical instruments, second-hand clothes, furniture and more (Fridays and Saturdays are best). Browsing St Patrick's St's brightly painted shopfronts with brass-lettered signs and ducking into the enticing little lanes is wonderful; and on a cold Cork day there's no better way to warm up than a steaming cup of liquid praline at French Church St's Ó Conaill Chocolates. Beyond the city limits, smacking your lips on the mythical Blarney Stone at 1446-built Blarney Castle is a time-honoured tradition. Tradition also prevails in Midleton at Jameson's whiskey distillery, which has been operating since the early 19th century and is still going strong (and yep, tours are followed by tastings). On Saturday mornings Midleton's artisan farmers market's brimming stalls and lively musicians showcase County Cork's rich regional produce. To explore more of the county, a two-hour drive southwest along the majestic Mizen Head Peninsula will bring you to the picturesque harbour hamlet of Crookhaven. Back in the city, tours of Cork's Beamish & Crawford Brewery also conclude with a taste test. Cork comes into its own after dark: the cobalt-blue Sin É, the Old Oak, O'Flaherty's and Brú Bar are among Cork's finest places for a pint, but you could crawl the pubs for weeks and still not run dry of places to try. Wherever you go, though, you'll want to try Murphy's, Cork's other hometown brew. Along the way, chances are you'll find your own favourite corner of Cork.

A clock tower rises above the city rooftops. **Oliver Strewe**

CITY HIGHLIGHTS

6th Floor Museum | A multimedia extravaganza examining President Kennedy's death and life.

Nasher Center | Modern art and sculpture among gardens and glass, an intriguing and meditative experience.

Bishop Arts District | Quirky galleries, cafés and antique stores in an old trolley stop community.

Mansion on Turtle Creek Restaurant | The ultimate opulence – splurge and experience fabulous food in a nationally known landmark setting.

Fort Worth Stockyards | Cows, cowboys and country dancing are all just 48km (30 miles) east of downtown Dallas.

The Perfect Day in
DALLAS

Lisa Dunford went to every barbecue joint she could find in her adopted state, Texas, for *USA 4*.

If I'm feeling decadent, I start my day with a cream puff or éclair from Breadwinners Bakery & Café in Uptown.

If I'm trying to be healthy I'll choose its vegetarian scramble instead – a great combination of artichoke hearts and cream cheese. After I'm fortified, I pop downtown to the 6th Floor Museum to see the latest special exhibit; a recent focus was on the press coverage of the John F Kennedy assassination. In the summer my next stop would be the Farmer's Market to feast on the sight of so many colourful ripe fruits and vegetables, and to check out the antiques in the adjacent building. In cooler weather I'd head further east to the Bishop Arts District (Bishop Ave at W Davis St) to see if I can add to my Fiestaware collection from one of the eclectic 'junque' dealer's shops. In the evening I'd have friends meet me at the picnic tables out back of the Ginger Man Pub for a happy-hour brew before deciding where to nosh at one of the many Uptown restaurants. So much food, so little time...

CITY HIGHLIGHTS

Red Fort | Ramble around this remarkable testament to Mughal India.

Museums & tombs | Explore star attractions such as the Crafts Museum, Humayun's Tomb and the National Museum.

Qutb Minar | Gape at this soaring victory tower, built to proclaim the arrival of Islam in India.

Jama Masjid | Marvel at India's biggest mosque.

Shopping | Sniff spices, browse for bangles and gobble *jalebis* (fried sweet 'squiggles') in Old Delhi's rambunctious bazaars.

The Perfect Day in
DELHI

Even after 20 visits (and four years' residence), **Sarina Singh** still can't get enough of India.

Destiny has been kind and brought me back to my motherland, India, at least once a year for the past 15 years. I have spent many, many months in Delhi and each time I return here – increasingly convinced that I've unpeeled the multi-layered capital to its elusive core – a brand new layer presents itself, leaving me yet again with more questions than answers...

It's largely this enigma that makes the subcontinent an eternal work-in-progress for even the most travelled traveller. My trips to Delhi often kick off with a jet-lagged ramble through the colonnaded familiarity of Connaught Place. Here I have the opportunity to 'subcontinentalise' myself at a languid pace before plunging into the raw hullabaloo of one of my favourite areas – the old city. After fuelling up on caffeine and croissants at one of the Big Circle's iridescent little cafés, I hop into an autorickshaw and rattle my way to Shahjahanabad, the erstwhile walled city. A nose-numbing pastiche of fumes, flowers, urine and spices swiftly lets me know I've reached my destination. I begin with a visit to the mighty Jama Masjid, imagining the atmosphere when the courtyard is filled with 25,000 worshippers. From the mosque I wend my way through the people-packed bazaars of the dusty old city, which flogs everything from sweet-scented oils to jingle-jangling anklets.

A few hours here leave me in a giddy daze, and although it's always a relief to flee the pandemonium of the old city, the memories I form here blaze brightest long after I've left India's shores. By now I'm famished and usually have potato-stuffed *dosas* (lentil-flour pancakes) dancing in my head: deciding where to satiate my craving is, thankfully, a no-brainer: Janpath's Saravana Bhavan, of course. After downing *dosas*, I often cut across to the adjacent Janpath (Tibetan) Market for a bit of knick-knack shopping. However, if the crush of humanity has left me ragged, I cruise over to the blissfully calm Crafts Museum to peruse the galleries and watch visiting artisans turn mud into masterpieces.

A woman's smiling face stands out from the piles of coloured fabrics at her stall. **Palani Mohan**

The Perfect Day in
DJENNÉ

Africa entices **Anthony Ham**, contributor to *Africa on a Shoestring*, into a yearly extended visit.

I'm not normally the world's earliest riser, but I make an exception in Djenné, especially if it's Monday. As close to sunrise as I can manage, I make for the Grande Mosquée, one of Africa's most spectacular and unusual landmarks, where the morning light is magical.

Already, stallholders mark out their patch of sand for a frenetic day's trading and I find a discreet vantage point from which to watch this exceptionally colourful passing parade. By mid-morning the market's in full swing and I'm in among it, using all of the few words of Bambara I know to haggle, seeking refuge from the pungent smells and generally flying high on the joy of being

surrounded by this very African market. Another Djenné awaits beyond the market, so I leave the crowds and lose myself in the antique, labyrinthine World Heritage-listed Old Town where architectural mud flourishes abound. Here, vignettes of African village life survive – two old men silently regard the world with the impenetrable gaze of the ancients, women gather water at the well, young girls in all their finery hurry to market. In my wanderings, I drop by Pama Sinatoa to watch the age-old art of making *bogolan* (mud) cloth and possibly buy one or two pieces as a keepsake for those days when the gentle charms

of Djenné are a nostalgic memory. The beautiful House of the Traditional Chief is always on my daily rounds but today I leave it behind quicker than I'd like and head for the nearby riverbank. Here, I am reminded that Djenné is an island and the sight of locals from outlying villages ferrying their produce to and fro is one that keeps me occupied for hours. Whether I return to the market, ponder the historically significant archaeological site of Jenné-Jeno or simply wander at will through the Old Town, I usually decide to extend my stay so that I can look forward to a Tuesday, when I have Djenné all to myself.

CITY HIGHLIGHTS

Burj al-Arab | Dubai's iconic hotel is a must-see.

Dubai Museum | A fascinating way to appreciate just how far (and how fast!) the city's progressed.

Souk shopping | Everything from 24-carat gold to mosque alarm clocks.

Bastakia Quarter | Wonderful windtower buildings in a tranquil setting.

Sheikh Zayed Rd | Quickly becoming Vegas without the gambling.

The Perfect Day in
DUBAI

A recent former resident of Dubai, **Terry Carter** is the author of the *Dubai* and *Best of Dubai* guides.

My perfect day usually involves showing guests around the city and nothing goes down better than starting the day with a dip in the Gulf, complete with an uninterrupted view of the Burj al-Arab from the beach at Jumeirah.

The next stop is always a step back in history with a trip to the Dubai Museum. Suitably amused and impressed, my guests are keen to keep the heritage theme happening so we'll take a walk through the Bastakia area and down to the Heritage and Diving Village. After a bite to eat it's off to Deira City Centre to start comparing rug prices before heading to the Gold Souq as it inshallah (God willing!) gets a little cooler. As everyone is always keen to keep shopping, we'll head to Souq Madinat Jumeirah, where my hidden agenda is scoring my favourite spot outside at Bahri Bar, with its unsurpassed views of Mina A' Salam and the Burj al-Arab. After a couple of sunset drinks it's generally off to one of my favourite Moroccan restaurants, usually Tagine, so my guests can have some *sheesha* (tobacco smoked through a water pipe) afterwards in the atmospheric Courtyard outside. If the weather's cool enough, we'll then head to Sho Cho, where the DJ keeps the tunes in time with the breaking waves and then kick on to Boudoir where bottles of spirits and dancers share the tabletops.

CITY HIGHLIGHTS

Edinburgh Castle | Still interesting after all these years.

Royal Yacht *Britannia* | A fascinating insight into what holidays are like when you're the Queen.

Underground Edinburgh | Visit Mary King's Close, or take a guided tour of the South Bridge vaults; spine-tinglingly creepy.

Museum of Scotland | Check out fantastic architecture as well as interesting exhibits – don't miss the miniature coffins discovered on Arthur's Seat in 1836.

Cramond | Wait for a sunny day and take a picnic lunch to this picture-postcard riverside village on the edge of the city.

The Perfect Day in
EDINBURGH

Neil Wilson is an Edinburgh resident and author of around 45 guidebooks, including *Edinburgh*.

Breakfast may be the best meal of the day, but you don't want to rush into it, especially in Edinburgh where the bars don't close until well after midnight.

So then, a longish lie-in followed by a walk to shake off the cobwebs – a stroll through Princes St Gardens followed by a stiff climb up to the Castle Esplanade should do it. Then down the scenic cobbled canyon of the Royal Mile to find a café where I can comfortably slump over coffee and newspapers for an hour or so. Then I might make yet another visit to the Museum of Scotland – I've been visiting regularly since it opened and still haven't seen everything. Or, if it's after noon on a weekday, nip into the Surgeons Hall museums for a look at the creepy but always fascinating Burke and Hare exhibit. If I'm feeling lazy, I would spend a whole afternoon browsing the second-hand bookshops in the West Port, or if energetic, I would get out the bike and cycle along the Water of Leith Walkway to the Pentland Hills (one of Edinburgh's great joys is its closeness to the countryside). In the evening, it's great to meet friends for a sampling session at the Malt Whisky Society rooms, followed by a seafood dinner at Fishers or Skippers in Leith. And then there are those late-opening pubs to think about again…

The Perfect Day in

ESSAOUIRA

Paula Hardy is a former resident of Libya and the author of *Morocco*, among many other guides.

It's a hot and sunny day in Essaouira and seagulls freewheel against a canvas of the most perfect, luminous shade of blue.

I can just see a sliver of the sun-spotted sea over the neighbours' rooftops. A hearty breakfast of steaming coffee, hot Moroccan pancakes slathered in honey, and a bowl of chilled fresh fruit on the terrace has to be one of life's most satisfying experiences – one that can easily stretch half the day. Oh, OK, I have to do something I guess. I would head straight to the beach: in winter when it's fresh and windy I can walk for miles along yawning wide beaches, the smack of salty air on my face. In summer

there's a whole other scene – the surfers are out in force, the sunbeds are full of lounge lizards and kids are up to their elbows in sandpits. A horse or camel trek can also be great fun and it gets you well out of the claustrophobic medina and into the pretty countryside. On other days I hook up with friends for some mad quad-biking. Lunch is always an easy affair in a beachfront café or even better at the portside snack stalls where you can buy your own fish, fried or grilled on the spot. In the evening the action moves back to the medina for the evening rush between 17:00 and 20:00. This is when the town is at its liveliest and I love

poking around the hidden nooks and crannies – like the little bric-a-brac auction opposite the fish market or the glittering windows of the gold souk. Then a rendezvous at Taros Cafe for a glass of chilled white wine on the roof terrace. For more romantic assignations, enjoy a beer on the ramparts watching the sun go down before a deliciously intimate dinner in Villa Maroc.

The fascinating old waterfront city of Essaouira hides behind stout ramparts that glow in unbeatable sunsets. **John Elk III**

CITY HIGHLIGHTS

Chiesa di San Miniato al Monte | Marvelling at both the jewel-like Romanesque church and its stunning views of Florence.

Giardino di Boboli | Strolling the sculpted paths of this monumental Renaissance garden.

Basilica di San Lorenzo | Meditating on the almost musical harmonies of Brunelleschi's interior.

Oltrarno | Escaping the crowded Duomo-Signoria nexus into the sleepier quarters across the Arno.

Piazza della Signoria | Taking morning coffee on the world's most civilised public space.

The Perfect Day in
FLORENCE

Robert Landon is a reporter, food, art and travel writer, and multiple Lonely Planet author.

It's April, and a week of rain has polished the skies and turned the hillsides a vital shade of green.

This particular morning is cloudless, and from my balcony I can look up the Arno to the Appenines, whose distant, plum-coloured peaks are visible for the first time since my arrival. Once again I understand that Renaissance painters did not idealise the Tuscan landscape; they merely neatened it up a little. I meet two friends – first-timers here – on Piazza della Signoria, that most human of spaces. I let them gush until Bruno, curator at the Uffizi, ushers us into his museum. It's closed Tuesdays, but another

friend has made calls, and as a result we can spend great stretches of time in front of Giottos, Boticellis, and da Vincis. Brains hot with art, we cross Ponte Vecchio to walk the cool, sculpted paths of the Boboli gardens. Then I surprise my hungry guests with a spread of Tuscan cheeses, meats, and Chiantis, which caterers have set out on the lawn of the Belvedere Palace. We eat with Florence laid out before us. After digesting and dozing in the shade, we head into the hillside orchards that, on this side of the river, reach down almost to the heart of Florence. Nature (blue cypress ordered into rows) and Art (ancient towers wild with vines)

are impossible to untangle. Later, we will dine exceedingly well outdoors on Piazza Santo Spirito, and then wander the knot of streets around the Palazzo Vecchio. However, this highly aesthetic day peaks at dusk when, from the steps of Chiesa di San Miniato, we watch the blushing Duomo succumb to the first long, mild evening of the year.

The Perfect Day in
GALWAY

Catherine Le Nevez has travelled at every opportunity since her wanderlust kicked in at age four.

Arty and bohemian, Galway (Gaillimh) is legendary for its energetic entertainment scene.

Even when it's wet (but especially when it's not) this city's curved cobblestone streets are filled with a frenzy of fiddles, banjos, bagpipes, tin whistles, guitars and traditional Irish *bodhrán* (drums), as spirited street performers, jugglers, painters, puppeteers and magicians in outlandish masks and costumes enchant passers-by. Colourfully painted pubs and quaint hole-in-the-wall cafés clustered throughout the centre spill out onto the pavements. Narrow shops display heavy hand-knitted Aran sweaters and handcrafted Claddagh rings. Bright terrace houses are stacked with second-hand and new books. Holistic healers conduct energy workshops. Mystics perform tarot readings. Farmers in Wellington boots unload fresh-out-of-the-ground parsnips, potatoes and carrots (still covered in soil) onto long trestle tables. Stalls sizzle up vegetarian feasts at the weekend markets. Bakeries are piled high with Irish and continental breads. Sprawling superpubs with winding staircases serve frothy pints of Guinness and tall glasses of Irish coffee warmed up even more with a hit of whiskey. Bridges arc over the salmon-filled River Corrib.

Intriguing museums, stone cathedrals, an inner-city castle and the remains of the medieval town walls bring the city's history to life. A long promenade leads to the seaside suburb of Salthill, where the moon's glow at night illuminates Galway Bay. And the barren, windswept Aran Islands, deep forests, misty lakes, quartzite peaks and green marble quarries in the nearby Connemara region, and the plunging Cliffs of Moher are only a day trip away. To top it off Galway hosts a heap of festivals from literature and the arts to horse-racing carnivals and a celebration of the bay's oyster harvest. But really, any day in and around Galway is a top one.

The Perfect Day in
GLASGOW

Alan Murphy, the main author of the *Scotland* guide, hopes one day to write a Good Pub guide.

I start my day in Glasgow full of expectation – this city always surprises and rarely disappoints.

Belly rumbling, I head for Cafe Lava, a tiny off-the-beaten-track café dishing out home cooking (great black pudding) and the best coffee in the city. Then my favourite attraction beckons – the Burrell Collection – where I randomly pick a part of the museum to explore. This is one of the best museums in Britain and the 'greenhouse effect' from the floor-to-ceiling windows always blows me away. Afterwards I head to the Clyde for a ride along the river that built Glasgow – its fascinating industrial heritage is being rejuvenated for tourism at an astonishing pace. I arrive at Clydebuilt: the museum's absorbing displays relay a fascinating heritage. On the way back I stop off in the West End for a drink at the Loft and some traditional Scottish cooking at the Bothy. Then it's straight to the leafy East End and Glasgow Cathedral, whose imposing interior conjures up medieval might and always brings out the goose bumps. I then walk to the Barras, Glasgow's legendary flea market for a slightly more modern-day Glaswegian experience. It may look shabby, but this place is the soul of the city and I'm left smiling at the wittiness of the traders long after I leave (when I've finally interpreted their 'weedgie' accent!). I make a beeline for Merchant City and admire the crumbling edifices left from the days when the Tobacco Lords were wallowing in their extravagant, cancer-inducing wealth. I head to Blackfriars – it specialises in cask ales – for a real Scottish brew and then move onto cosy Rab Ha's for another drink by the fire. At Brutti Ma Buoni's, my favourite bar-restaurant, I have 'an ugly but good' pizza. Lastly, to King Tut's for a gig – Snow Patrol rock the house and I wonder how I can go about extending my stay in this wonderful city.

CITY HIGHLIGHTS

Old Quarter | Put away the map, and explore the bustling streets and lanes of the Old Quarter.

Temple of Literature | Take time out from the din of motorbikes and horns and enjoy the serenity.

Bia hoi | Tuck into some of Hanoi's famous 'fresh beer' at a beer hall or street corner in the Old Quarter, and make new friends in the process.

Uncle Ho's Mausoleum | Pay your respects to the father of modern Vietnam.

Pho Nha Tho | When the sightseeing is done, stop here for classy cuisine and retail therapy.

The Perfect Day in
HANOI

Journalist, photographer and *Laos* guide author **Andrew Burke** has lived in Asia since 2001.

There's something about Hanoi that encourages early rising. It might be that most Vietnamese seem pathologically incapable of sleeping beyond about 05:00, no matter how much *bia hoi* (draught beer) and rice wine they put away the night before.

And so I try (OK, yes, only a couple of times a week) to prise myself out of bed, shoulder my camera and wander down to Hoan Kiem Lake as early as possible. The benefits are soon apparent; traffic in the Old Quarter is quiet, a ghostly blue-grey mist hovers above the lake and elderly Hanoians practice their distinctive floppy t'ai chi in slow rotation around its perimeter. As the sun rises I'll wander through the Old Quarter, watching the city wake up along streets lined with trees and crumbling buildings of yellow stucco, eventually stopping for breakfast of *pho* and a fresh, fluffy baguette. Suitably fortified, I'll head out to the Ho Chi Minh Mausoleum before the crowds arrive. I've seen Bac Ho before, but with rumours he might be about to get his wish and be buried, I figure it's time for one last peek. I love the romance and history of Hanoi and few places encompass it quite like the Temple of Literature. Sitting here with a book is the perfect respite from the buzz of the city, and eating lunch at nearby KOTO satisfies both my hunger and my desire to aid the less fortunate of the city. In the afternoon I might just wander down to Pho Nha Tho for some shopping and a drink while watching the shadows of St Joseph's Cathedral grow longer, before heading back into the Old Quarter for *bia hoi* with friends. Dinner at the Culi Cafe (40 Luong Ngoc Quyen) makes a tasty change from Vietnamese food, and a stroll down to Highway 4 for rice wine on the roof (get there before 23:00 and hustle upstairs) will ensure I won't be up early tomorrow.

The Perfect Day in
HAVANA

Cuba author **Conner Gorry** first visited the country in 1993, and has been coming back ever since.

If there's electricity and running water when dawn breaks on Havana, my day is off with a bang. I'll start with a typical Cuban breakfast of teeny cups of sweet, dark espresso, toast and a tropical fruit shake.

Cranking on high octane caffeine, I rush to the street to see that my chariot has arrived: a gloriously uncrowded (now there's a fantasy!) *camello*, one of Havana's infamous giant buses that often cram in up to 350 people. It's a sweaty, lumbering ride to the Capitolio and Havana's heart, but becomes pleasantly bearable once the *compañero* at my elbow decides to brush up on his English and regale me with tales of old New York. Folks like him – who fled to Cuba rather than from it after the revolution – intrigue me. I'm in the zone, trading witty remarks with the jineteros (hustlers) and cigar peddlers. I finally make my way to the astounding Capitolio or enjoy the view from the top of the Bacardí building. There's always something different happening in Havana if you know where to look – today it's an emerging artists exhibit at the spiffy Museo Nacional de Bellas Artes. Hunger comes upon me, so I grab a *cajita* (little box) stuffed with pork, *congrí* (local dish of rice, beans and banana) and salad at my favourite take-out place on the edge of the Barrio Chino before doing a little shopping and character research along San Rafael – the chaotic, exotic pedestrian boulevard that cuts through Centro Habana. The heat is oppressive and I'll need a disco nap if I want to make tonight's concert: either X Alfonso at the University or Los Van Van at the Casa de la Música – tough choice. Joining the throngs flagging down a classic jalopy that will take us across town for 10 pesos, I plan dinner while eavesdropping on two beauties gossiping about their boyfriends. I decide on the special at the very retro La Roca in Vedado. Then I'm off to shake my booty. After the post-concert party, watching the sun rise from the Malecón provides a lyrical finale to the day.

CITY HIGHLIGHTS

Sea Horse | A Helsinki favourite since the 1930s that hasn't changed its décor or its filling, traditional food.

Harbour | Head to Suomenlinna fortress, to the zoo or to an island restaurant.

Kotiharjun Sauna | Sweat it out with the locals at this historic sauna.

Beer-swilling | Enjoy the long summer sunshine at one of the city's great beer terraces.

Temppeliaukio | Catch a concert at this spectacular church hewn out of bedrock.

The Perfect Day in
HELSINKI

Andy Symington wrote the book on Finland – the Lonely Planet guidebook, that is.

Finns are among the world's biggest coffee drinkers, so, not surprisingly, cafés are something they do particularly well.

Some of my favourites are along the Esplanade that leads down to the harbour. So, it's a strong brew at the Strindberg, accompanied by a cardamom-flavoured *pulla* (sweet bread ring). From here, it's a short stroll down to the busy *kauppatori* (market square), where fresh produce is still sold off boats moored at the quay in summer. Helsinki is a harbour city par excellence, so I jump on a boat to Suomenlinna island, the 'fortress of Finland'. If the weather's nice, I take a picnic. Back

in town, I head to Senate Square, the neoclassical heart of Helsinki to check out its cathedral. Nearby, the Uspenski cathedral is the Orthodox equivalent, and clearly has Russian architectural influences. Suitably inspired, I continue the theme with a light lunch at one of the many excellent Russian restaurants. Art is on the afternoon menu and, depending on my mood, it's off to the Ateneum for my favourites from Finland's golden age or to jazzy Kiasma, the contemporary art equivalent and the place to be seen. Thirsty work, galleries, so in the late afternoon it's time for a Lapin Kulta beer at Vltava. Now it's time to get

body and soul together. To find that inner peace I head straight for the excellent Kotiharjun Sauna, a historical sauna that's seen more than a drop or two. I sweat it out in the nude with stoic Finns and get a scrub down from the grandmotherly attendant. Then it's back to town with a hunger that can only be satisfied with seafood at an island restaurant in Helsinki harbour. Boathouse is my favourite. Appetite satisfied, I check out Tavastia, a legendary rock venue, or head for one of the trendy bars around Iso Roobertinkatu. Later, you'll find me on the dancefloor in a club – Uniq, perhaps – or chilling out, literally, in the ice bar!

Early morning light over the marina at Pohjoisranta near Senate Square. **Jonathan Smith**

The Perfect Day in

HO CHI MINH CITY

Journalist, photographer and *Laos* guide author **Andrew Burke** has lived in Asia since 2001.

My top day in Ho Chi Minh City (still called Saigon by its denizens) begins with a bowl of *pho* (noodle soup) from a streetside stall in the Pham Ngu Lao area.

With camera to hand, I'd then set forth into the traffic and wander up to Cong Vien Van Hoa Park for a stroll among the exercising locals, before continuing on to the War Remnants Museum. With all that military hardware on display, at first glance this museum can look like a celebration of war. It's not. Each time I visit, it's a sobering but intensely worthwhile experience. The nearby Reunification Palace speaks to the same turbulent period of modern history but in more extravagant language. I love the classic '60s architecture, the furniture that's remained unchanged since 1975, and the shaky television pictures of tanks bursting through gates that run through my head while sitting in the grounds. Saigon is all about street food, so I'll walk down to Ben Thanh Market and follow my nose to the food vendors for lunch with a *bia hoi* (draught beer) or two. My nose will also lead me to the market's coffee merchants, a tasting session and yet another kilogram or two of the best arabica. In the afternoon I'll sit in a café (the long-running Givral, perhaps), read the paper and conserve energy for the evening... Ah, the evening in Saigon! I'll meet friends at the Saigon Saigon Bar for sundowners and discussion of the latest and greatest Vietnamese beach resort, before moving on to dinner at one of the Dong Khoi restaurants (probably Quan An Ngon if we feel like local cuisine, or Augustin for delicious, cheap French food). Dinner is followed by a round of cocktails at trendy Q-Bar, where, suitably lubricated, I might allow myself to be persuaded into a dancing mission to Apocalypse Now. The final act is a *xe om* (motorbike taxi) trip back to Pham Ngu Lao, a great way to clear the head.

CITY HIGHLIGHTS

Victoria Peak | Look down on the city from on high.

Star Ferry | Get a sea-level look at Hong Kong's skyscraping shoreline.

Temple St Night Market | Buy your way through cheap stalls and fill up on street food.

Trams | Take a slow ride across Hong Kong Island and watch the street life from a double-decker tram.

Man Mo Temple | Admire the oversized incense cones and calm your spirits.

The Perfect Day in
HONG KONG

Paul Smitz's numerous Lonely Planet writing credits include *Southeast Asia on a Shoestring.*

I get up early and take a leisurely walk through Hong Kong Park, where I'm entranced by the slow-motion grace of t'ai chi practitioners and the wonderful birds in the Edward Youde Aviary.

Now I'm ready for a hearty breakfast (invariably involving eggs) in one of Central's cafés, somewhere with an interesting crowd like Eating Plus in the IFC Mall. After breakfast I head outside and squint up at the bullet-shaped outline of the city's tallest building, Two IFC, before jamming myself among commuters for the trip across spectacular Victoria Harbour to Kowloon on the ungainly Star Ferry. I arrive in Tsim Sha Tsui and meander along

its promenade to admire the view back across to Hong Kong Island. I may even duck into the Hong Kong Space Museum to take in its enormous planetarium or a new IMAX film. Next I walk up the Golden Mile (Nathan Rd) to breathe in the commercial chaos and pay my respects to the authentically decrepit Chungking Mansions (a favourite place to stay) before diving into Tsim Sha Tsui MTR station. I catch a train two stops north to Yau Ma Tei, where the tourist traffic is almost nonexistent and I can wander down Temple St and observe the streetlife as stallholders set up the Night Market. Hungry now, I'll ride the MTR south again and

enter the basement of the Kowloon Hotel, where I've booked myself a fabulous dim sum banquet at Hoi Yat Heen. I ride the Star Ferry back across the harbour (once is never enough) and catch the steep Peak Tram for fantastic late-afternoon views from Victoria Peak. Then I'll ride the tram back down and make for the Central Escalator, which trundles me up through the Mid-Levels to catch glimpses of Hong Kong life through the windows of the bars and residential apartments crowding around it. Finally I disappear into the alleys of Lan Kwai Fong to celebrate the day with numerous drinks and some decent after-hours food.

Buzzing with activity at any time of day, Queen's Rd lights up with neon at dusk. Ray Laskowitz

The Perfect Day in
HONOLULU & WAIKIKI

Hawaiian native **Luci Yamamoto** is the author of *Hawaii: the Big Island*.

In Honolulu it's impossible to oversleep: the sun's shining practically from dawn! I pack a picnic lunch and walk the length of Waikiki Beach towards Diamond Head.

The beach is actually peaceful if you beat the crowds. When I reach the end at Kapiolani Park, I unroll my *goza* (straw mat) and relax, reading under a tree, tossing a football, or visiting the adjacent zoo. Waikiki might be over-the-top touristy but it's fun for people-watching. So I stroll back along the main thoroughfare, Kalakaua Ave, watching an endless stream of bikini tops and surfer shorts, ABC Stores, pale flesh fried pink, trendy Japanese youths and pristine Cinderella wedding gowns. In the afternoon I head to Ala Moana Center, full of designer boutiques and only-in-Hawaii shops, to satisfy my occasional craving to splurge. Can't miss the sweet-sour-salty island treats at Crack Seed Center! While the Waikiki crowd is mostly tourists, Ala Moana Center is jammed with Honolulu folks – it's an ideal place to listen to pidgin and observe local society. I end the day by watching canoe paddlers practice in the Ala Wai Canal, followed by a sunset swim at Sans Souci (Kaimana) beach. The water is spectacular, especially in the mornings and evenings, when the sunlight is angled just so. Another favourite is Ala Moana Beach Park, which cannot be beaten for its convenient location and lap swimming. For a casual dinner, I head to Shokudo (Ala Moana Center, 1585 Kapiolani Blvd), a hip restaurant and bar with Japanese small plates like nowhere else. For a splurge, I head to Indigo, an Asian-fusion icon in the latest hip neighbourhood, Chinatown. If I still have enough energy for a drink, Waikiki is the main late-night spot (even retail shops stay open till 22.00 or 23.00). But I come to Honolulu to chill out. So I'll probably just savour the balmy, sweater-free night and fall asleep to dream of another languid day.

CITY HIGHLIGHTS

Aya Sofya | Marvel at one of the world's great buildings and its extraordinary dome.
Grand Bazaar & Tahtakale District | Join the crush and lose yourself in this splendid shopping mecca.
Istiklal Caddesi | Visit the city's 'main drag' and its thriving eating, bar and club scene. At its best in the evenings and on weekends.
Bosphorus Cruise | Take a day-trip up this busy waterway and get to grips with Istanbul's geography.
Topkapi Palace | Join the throngs for a glimpse of the Ottoman Empire at its finest; the Harem is a must-see.

The Perfect Day in
ISTANBUL

Istanbul author **Verity Campbell** once lived in a decrepit but charming apartment in the city.

My day always starts with pebble- or chestnut-throwing around the fountain at Sultanahmet Parki (I have a one-year-old), with the Blue Mosque behind one shoulder and Aya Sofya behind the other – what a location!

We love chatting to the costumed juice sellers as they preen themselves for the full day of photography ahead (does my moustache look big in this?). Chestnuts exhausted, I head to Aya Sofya, my favourite building in the city, if not the world. From there I walk along the ancient Roman road, Divan Yolu, to enter the Grand Bazaar from its southern end to travel with the foot traffic downhill towards the Golden Horn. My well-worn path meanders through the glittering gold arcade and past the chintz and carpets, but I never miss poking my head into the gorgeous pink Zincirli Han. However, I don't shop in the Grand Bazaar – I shop in Tahtakale as do many locals – the crush can be overbearing, especially on Saturdays. From here I head over to join the throngs along Beyoglu's teeming promenade, Istiklal Caddesi. Beyoglu is the heart of modern Istanbul and home to a thriving arts scene, bars and some of the best restaurants in the city. You haven't seen Istanbul until you've explored Beyoglu. For dinner I meet up with friends at our long-time favourite, Haci Abdullah, before heading down Sofyali Sokak. Tonight we choose Badehane, a laneway watering hole that's a regular choice on low-key evenings. We're priming ourselves for tomorrow's night out at Soho Supper Club, a minimalist bar popular with a mixed crowd. Or maybe 5 Kat? The options are endless.

Whirling dervishes are just one must-see attraction among Istanbul's fabulous nightlife. **Scott Barbour**

CITY HIGHLIGHTS

Jaisalmer Fort | Amble down the alleys of this goliathan, endangered monument, still teeming with residents.

Rajmahal | Explore beauties and oddities in a former maharaja's palace.

Camel safari | Cushion your bum, don your shades and voyage into the deserts beyond.

Kuldhara | A look at a local village that has starred in a film or two; you can camel trek here too.

Akal Wood Fossil Park | Imagine what must have once been, 180 million years ago.

The Perfect Day in
JAISALMER

Susan Derby co-wrote *India* and rates India as one of her two favourite places in the world.

The desert morning air is clear and crispy cool. I wrap up in a wool shawl and wander through the almost-quiet narrow streets.

At the market stalls near the Jaisalmer Fort entrance, I buy some fruit for my day then duck into the simple Llasa/Joshi Café & German Bakery for eggs, fresh baked bread and a glass of warming *chai*. Fort bound, I pass the Bhang Shop and briefly consider...nah, way too early. Before tackling the fort's maze of cows, people and shops fronted by wowing tapestries, satiny bedspreads and silver bangles, I stop and listen. From the steps next to Rajmahal arise the foot-tapping sounds of local percussion musicians.

Waiting their turn for the limelight, children close by prepare to walk a tightrope. Later, back in town, my appetite will settle for nothing less than a gratifying thali at Chandan Shree Restaurant. I overdo it, of course, and wade molasses-like through the now-busy Bhatia Market. I think about heading to 300-year-old Salim Singh-ki-Haveli. It's a beautiful building, but the real temptation now is the Ayurveda Hub nearby, which offers a menu of yummy treatments. A massage will better serve me later in the week though, when I'll be on a camel safari – my aching self will certainly need help. Back in the

fort, I spend time in the Jain temples complex, in mesmerised mode. I eventually find myself at Ristorante Italiano La Purezza in the early evening. What it lacks in cosy ambience it makes up for in stellar sunset views. The sinking orange ball and the glow it casts over the sweep of Jaisalmer below are magic pure and simple. Dinner with a friend is perfectly atmospheric at the abuzz Trio, where a band of Rajasthani musicians complement the slow dance on my taste buds with their rhythms. It's early to dreams for me tonight then, with visions of bopping camels, sweeping sands and starstruck nights in the Great Thar Desert.

CITY HIGHLIGHTS

Yad Vashem | Memorial dedicated to the six million Jews who perished in the Holocaust.

Tmol Shilshom | Kick back with a coffee and a cake in this bohemian café.

Temple Mount | Join the throngs of pilgrims marching to the most sacred place in Jerusalem.

Museum on the Seam | Understand the Arab-Jewish conflict by taking a peek inside this museum.

Via Dolorosa | Jesus' ancient route on his way to Calvary, culminating at the breathtaking Church of the Holy Sepulchre.

The Perfect Day in
JERUSALEM

Michael Kohn made his first visit to his favourite destination, Jerusalem, at 15.

In Jerusalem's Old City, the best part of the day is waking up.

There's no need for an alarm clock when the discordant bells of the Church of the Holy Sepulchre resonate across the rooftops. Almost instinctively I climb the steep staircase to the roof of my guesthouse and gaze out over the four quarters of the walled city, the sun rising over the Mount of Olives and gleaming off the gold-plated Dome of the Rock. Still rubbing the sleep from my eyes I make my way towards the Temple Mount, stopping briefly for a breakfast snack at Bonker's Bagels in the Jewish Quarter. As the sparrows flit and chirp noisily over the cypress trees, our group is led to the Temple Mount, the sacred site containing the Al-Aqsa Mosque and the rock made holy by both Abraham and the Prophet Mohammed. After a brief, self-guided tour I sharpen my elbows and plunge headlong into the Arab souk, absorbing its energy and breathing in its spice-laden air. I stand back and watch the Arab traders as they go about their business – haggling, puffing on *sheeshas* (water pipes) and stroking their whiskers while they sip thimbles of Turkish coffee. When it comes time for lunch I make my way up to the Christian quarter to dine on the rooftop terrace at Papa Andrea's.

The food is piping hot, the portions big and the views spectacular. Rested, my next point of interest is one of Christendom's most sanctified places: the Church of the Holy Sepulchre. If it's Friday, the Old City starts to shut down for Shabbat around 15:00, but this is by no means a reason to escape. On the contrary, Shabbat in the Holy City can be a magical experience if you've got a family to share it with. Having pre-arranged a Shabbat dinner, I head down to the Kotel (the Western or Wailing Wall), watch the Jewish faithful dance and sing in circles, and then slip away for a cornucopia of kosher delights.

The Al-Aqsa Mosque and Dome of the Rock is one of Old Jerusalem's finest attractions. **Oliver Strewe**

CITY HIGHLIGHTS

Apartheid Museum & Constitution Hill | A worthy combined introduction to the city. The hill is the site of the Constitutional Court, born in the country's democratic era.

Cradle of Humankind | A World Heritage site with about 40 significant fossil areas.

Newtown | The nexus of the urban regeneration project, including the Gauteng Tourism Authority's new headquarters.

Township experience | Take a tour or explore on your own.

Street culture | Escape the shopping malls at 7th St Melville, Grant Ave Norwood and 4th Ave Parkhurst.

The Perfect Day in
JOHANNESBURG

Joburg-born **Alistair Simmonds** has been writing about travel in South Africa since 1998.

Johannesburg is a city of cars. Behind the wheel, this fast, sequestered and strange metropolis is mine.

As I drive, I see why Joburg, Jozi, Egoli or the City of Gold has a name for each of its faces; whether it's Chinatown in Bruma, Muslim Fordsburg or Black Soweto, each is defined by dynamic commercial and fashionable shifts. I head up to Northcliff for a view of the city, and notice how it boasts the world's largest urban forest (though it's barely able to attract residents to its sprawling public parks). I explore the mega-rich northern suburbs for a sobering dose of contradiction, where mansion fortresses lie minutes from the shacks of Alexandra township, and where inner-city nature reserves mingle with cellphone towers disguised as palm trees. I am drawn at once into the shebeens (drinking dens) of the township and just as quickly into Sandton City, the apotheosis of the shopping centre, that labyrinthine paean to consumerism that Joburg taught me not to hate. Here I witness how the new South African family has begun to redefine the country's divisions in terms of class, not race (Joburg shows this shift most glaringly). Once the stifle of the climate control gets to me, I escape to 7th St Melville for remnants of a street culture that, for now, has vanished from the city centre at night. So it's bookshops, bakeries and restaurants until Joburg falls into another night and starts to buzz, then it's Berlin Bar, the best spot on the strip. I head back via the shimmering Nelson Mandela Bridge, over the Witwatersrand. It was here that gold was discovered and where the name of the country's currency comes, so it's apt to finish up my visit to Johannesburg by going back to where it all began. North of the central business district, Newtown awaits, as does Carfax, a legendary mixed club that mixes it up and kicks down.

Durbar Square | Soak up the fantastic architecture at the stepped Maju Deval temple.

Old town | Explore the back streets around the market square of Asan Tole, north of Durbar Square.

Bodhnath | Let yourself be swept around Nepal's largest stupa and get a taste of Tibetan culture.

Thamel shopping | Trekking gear, books, CDs, *thangkas* (paintings) and tiger balm, along with a spare bag to carry them all in.

Patan | Back streets full of Buddhist *bahals* (courtyards) and the country's best museum.

The Perfect Day in
KATHMANDU

Nepal author **Bradley Mayhew** has been exploring the remoter parts of Asia since his college days.

Assuming I'm jet lagged and can face getting up at 07:00, I'd go for a wander around the backstreets between Thamel and Durbar Square, nibbling on a croissant picked up the night before at a Thamel bakery.

The streets are alive at this time of day with locals performing pujas and making offerings of marigolds, bananas, milk and coconut, topped off with a ring of the temple bell. Porters wait for customers at stepped temples and farmers set up their displays of carrots, lemons and curd. After an hour or so, I'd head back to Thamel for a leisurely late breakfast at Helena's rooftop restaurant and then browse the bookshops for obscure Tibetan titles or check out the latest canyoning, rafting or trekking trips on offer. Thamel grates after a while so taking a break from the tiger balm sellers and rickshaw-wallahs I'd head for the beautifully restored and totally serene Garden of Dreams or check out some of the amazing antique travel books in the mothballed Kaiser Mahal Library. In the late afternoon, I'd jump in a taxi to Bodhnath to join the elderly Tibetan pilgrims circumambulating the incredible stupa and then visit one or two of the monasteries to get my daily fix of Tibetan chanting and the smell of juniper incense. Back in Thamel, the evening gets kicked off by happy-hour cocktails at Maya Cocktail Bar and then comes the toughest decision of the day: dinner. Felafel and hummus at Nargila's? A Thai curry at Yin Yang? Or a steak sizzler at K2? Either way, on the way home, pick up half-price bakery goods after 21:00 for tomorrow's breakfast. And so it begins again...

CITY HIGHLIGHTS

Smithwicks Brewery | Queue at the gate early on midsummer mornings for one of just 50 free tickets to see where Kilkenny beer is made.

La Creperie | Sip phenomenal family-manufactured Moretti coffee flown in from Italy at this splendid hole-in-the-wall café.

Tynan's Bridgehouse | Savour perfectly poured pints, live music and great *craic* between the crooked walls of this 300-year-old pub.

Rinuccini Restaurant | Even if Rinuccini's signature lobster dish, *Spaghattini al Astici*, isn't on the menu, ask and you might be in luck.

Kilkenny Castle | Built in 1192 and still spectacular.

The Perfect Day in
KILKENNY

Catherine Le Nevez has travelled at every opportunity since her wanderlust kicked in at age four.

Is the Ireland of your imagination filled with massive medieval castles on the banks of a meandering river?

Steadfast stone churches and round-towered cathedrals? Steep 17th-century pedestrian passageways weaving between the city streets? Rows of colourful, terraced shopfronts? A legendary brewery wafting whiffs of hops (and, if you're able to score a ticket, an inside glimpse and tasting, too)? Jovial locals who stop you to chat in the street? Stone walled, emerald green fields stretching across the surrounding countryside? Cute-as-a-button B&Bs where you're treated like part of the family? Atmospheric three-centuries-old pubs with live Irish music? Quaint cafés and snazzy contemporary ones, as well as glamorous gastronomic restaurants that continue to amass awards? A hub of traditional crafts like pottery, knitting, goldsmithing and silversmithing, showcased in a series of studios in former castle stables? A crammed calendar of festivals from comedy to the full spectrum of the arts, to rhythm and roots music, to Frisbee tournaments? And, even if your time in Ireland's at a premium, do you imagine being just an easy couple of hours from Dublin? If – like this author – your dreams of Ireland conjure up all that and more, welcome to Chill Chainnigh, aka Kilkenny.

Colourful facades line John St in Kilkenny town. **Richard Cummins**

The Perfect Day in
KRAKÓW

Mara Vorhees has worked on seven Lonely Planet guides, including *Europe on a Shoestring*.

It's Sunday, and I start the day with a piping hot cappuccino at the bohemian Cafe Camelot. Properly fuelled up, I stroll across the Main Square as the Old Town begins to come to life.

I stop at St Mary's Church, or perhaps the Franciscan Church, to sit for a moment in quiet solitude, awestruck by the artistry of Stanisław Wyspia ski's stained-glass windows. If I'm so inspired, I may stay for a service, and engage in the centuries-old spiritual tradition I share with Polish Catholics. Afterwards, I walk down to Kazimierz, where Plac Nowy has come to life. I hunt for trash and treasure at the hustling, bustling flea market, and pick up a few ingredients for a picnic lunch. When my money is spent, I rent a bicycle at Krakow on Two Wheels (Kraków na Dwóch Kołach; ul Józefa) and pedal down to the Vistula River. I cruise along the bike path, which follows the river through Kazimierz, past Wawel Castle and out of the city centre. By the day's end, I make my way back to the centre. I am tempted to spend the evening hanging out in the atmospheric pubs around Plac Nowy. Instead, I enjoy one refreshing beer, then head back to the Old Town for dinner. I have a date to dine at Padre (cnr uls Wi lnej & Olszewskiego), in romantic vaulted cellars beneath an ancient monastery in the oldest part of Poland's beautiful royal city.

The serenity of St Mary's Church is illuminated at dusk. **Bruce Yuanyue Bi**

CITY HIGHLIGHTS

Chinatown | One minute you're contemplating life at a temple, the next you're squeezing past piles of shoes on Jl Petaling.

Masjid Jamek | Visit KL's stunning mosque and watch the sun set over its onion domes.

Little India | Sari stalls, superb food and the Saturday night market.

KL Tower | Spot your hotel from high above the chaos.

Food | Malay, Indian or Chinese – Kuala Lumpur has the best of three worlds.

The Perfect Day in
KUALA LUMPUR

Author of several Indonesia titles, **Patrick Witton** first donned a backpack in Asia at age three.

The best place to watch KL wake up is in Chinatown. At one of the streetside stalls on Jl Hang Lekir, I can see piles of mangosteens being carted while I'm downing a bowl of *juk* **(rice porridge) followed by a black coffee.**

Now fully charged, I can do a lap of Chinatown – no doubt discovering another tea shop or backstreet temple – then wander up past the Central Market and through to Masjid Jamek so I can take in the beauty of this century-old mosque. In order to continue the cruisy morn, I head over to the verdant Lake Gardens for a bit of a nature fix and a chance to visit the striking Islamic Arts Museum. Lunch beckons, so it's over to Little India for a South Indian lunch of rice, dhal and pickles served on a banana-palm plate. If the shopping bug bites, I get on the monorail to be transported to the megaplexes of Jl Bukit Bintang, KL's consumer core. Once the sun starts dropping it's time to head to the top of KL Tower for a knockout view across the city as it starts to twinkle. But where to for dinner? Back to Chinatown for Hokkien noodles and a chance to pick up some suspect DVDs? Over to Jl Alor for some chilli-grilled stingray? If it's Saturday night it's a no-brainer: straight over to the Little India night market, a frenetic mile of fantastic food.

CITY HIGHLIGHTS

Museo de Coca | Gain a fascinating insight into the legendary leaf.

Tailor-made clothes | Get a bargain-priced new suit or ball gown at one of La Paz's expert tailors.

Almuerzo | Treat yourself to a slap-up set lunch and be amazed at the price when the bill comes.

San Francisco | Shop till you drop at the market where you can find anything and everything.

Calle Sagárnaga | The main gringo alley has it all, from fruit smoothies to must-buy souvenirs.

The Perfect Day in
LA PAZ

Award-winning writer **David Atkinson** recently spent an extended period working in La Paz.

La Paz lives, breathes and survives on the street so there's nothing for it but to brace yourself and wade in. Personally I like to start the day with a hit of pure vitamin C.

Juice carts prowl the Prado, La Paz's main commercial drag, and I can get my fruity fix for just a few cents. A few cents more takes me right across town to the museum district of Calle Jaén, where the city's cultural district continues to reveal new attractions on each visit. Mid-morning and back on the streets, there's time to stop off at a streetside stall for a quick snack before crossing the Prado, catching a glimpse of the sun glancing off the facade of San Francisco Cathedral, and climbing Calle Sagárnaga. This entails diving into the seething mass of the backpacker district. Everyone is on the hustle here, so just go with it: bargain for a cool souvenir, negotiate the price of an excursion or check your email at a makeshift joint touting for new business. For lunch I might go gringo and munch through a traveller-friendly menu, or go native and grab a bargain set lunch around the corner on Calle Illampu. Either way it's going to be cheap but cheerful. The afternoon brings a fitting for some tailor-made clothes, browsing for cheap CDs and DVDs in the market and a lazy *cafe con leche* at one of my favourite coffee shops, Pepe's, while planning the night ahead. After dark the action moves west to the Sopocachi district, where the bars and restaurants around Plaza Avaroa have drinks, dancing and plenty of chances to fraternise with the locals well into the early hours.

CITY HIGHLIGHTS

The Strip | Live it up at glam casino hotels, megaresorts and ultra lounges.

Fremont St | Cruise the down 'n' dirty haunts of retro Glitter Gulch downtown.

Stratosphere | Almost fly atop the highest structure west of the Mississippi River.

Atomic Testing Museum | Look back to when mushroom clouds bloomed over the Nevada desert.

Leaving Las Vegas | Escape beyond the city limits to Hoover Dam, Red Rock Canyon, the Valley of Fire, Zion National Park, the Grand Canyon and Death Valley, each less than half a day's drive away.

The Perfect Day in
LAS VEGAS

Las Vegas author **Sara Benson**'s travel writing has featured in US papers from coast to coast.

Nobody's an early riser in Vegas. Shaking off the Rabelaisian fête of the night before, I get up just in time to make it into the breakfast buffet line, maybe at Le Village at Paris-Las Vegas, then take a free gambling lesson at one of the Strip's megaresort casinos.

I laze away the desert afternoon by the hotel pool or at a primo spa. As the sun starts to sink, it's time to zoom up the Stratosphere tower for thrill rides and drinks at the Top of the World lounge. Scoring a dinner reservation at Rosemary's justifies a big detour before heading back to the Strip. Then I let the gaming begin, eventually winding up downtown, where I get into an Old Vegas mood at the Golden Nugget, admire the vintage signs of the Neonopolis and duck into the back poker room at Binion's. After having the total Fremont St Experience, I head out to a nightclub like Ice. After hours, I drop by Mr Lucky's and play the rock 'n' roll slot machines at the Hard Rock before catching a little vampiric shut-eye back at my hotel. Why? Because at noon, it starts all over again.

Plaza de Armas | Step back in time at Lima's historical centre.

Museo Larco | Marvel at the enormous collection of ancient ceramics, textiles and metalwork, and an erotic art gallery, too.

Miraflores | Strut your stuff in Lima's shopping mecca, presided over by Huaca Pucllana, an ancient adobe pyramid dating from AD 500.

Barranco | Shake your booty till dawn in this arty modern *barrio* by the sea.

Pachacmac | Ramble in this mind-boggling ancient complex of temples, palaces and pyramids.

The Perfect Day in
LIMA

A traveller by passion and a writer by trade, **Sara Benson** has worked on over a dozen guidebooks.

Most Limeños would agree that a day without eating is like a day without life, so I start off at the city's top bakery, Panko's, where the shelves are filled with fresh sweet and savoury delights.

After gulping down a rich coffee I amble up past the Plaza San Martin, presided over by the Gran Hotel Bolivar, which shakes a mean pisco sour, the national cocktail. It's a bit early in the day for that, so I keep heading north onto Jiron de la Union, a pedestrian-only shopping street, which darts straight into the city's historical centre. It leads to the venerable Plaza de Armas, flanked by the Palacio de Gobierno, where Peru's president lives,

and La Catedral, where the remains of Spanish explorer Francisco Pizarro rest. A quick detour takes me on a guided tour of the ghoulish Museo de la Inquisición or over to the Museo Taurino, with its glorious relics of bullfights past. Then it's time for lunch at L'Eau Vive, a nonprofit restaurant inside a colonial mansion run by a French order of nuns. I devote the early afternoon to Peru's ancient civilizations at either the Museo Larco or the Museo de la Nación, either one an inexpensive taxi ride away from the city centre. Then before the sun sets, I'm off to the ritzy suburb of Miraflores for shopping and sunset views of the

Pacific Ocean, enjoyed from a pier-side table at La Rosa Náutica or the equally gourmand El Señorio del Sulco restaurant atop the cliffs. After dark, I speed down to Barranco, an artsy, eclectic *barrio* (neighbourhood) best known for its live-music clubs and DJs that keep the beats going till the break of dawn.

A candlelit procession makes its way around the Plaza de Armas. **Wes Walker**

The Perfect Day in
LISBON

Robert Landon is a food, art and travel writer, and the author of the *Portuguese* phrasebook.

It's June and I am catching the earliest part of morning; the sunlight is the best thing about Lisbon even if it's left me sunburned in odd places after a clothing-optional day on one of the southern beaches.

The sun is shining into the Baixa café where I stand taking my *pão* (bread) and *café com leite*. A handwritten sign behind the bar advises patrons that snails are now available, while outside, the city's distinctive trams rumble through the tight grid of 18th-century streets. Soon I am hopping on Tram No 28, which heads uphill, glancing past Lisbon's Romanesque cathedral with its fortress-like walls, and then slicing through the Alfama – the maze of streets and stairways that, since Arab times, has cascaded down the hill towards the Rio Tejo. Further up looms Castelo São Jorge, whose crenulated walls and towers are shorthand for the city itself. Now we're passing a series of plazas, some with glittering views of the river, and several crowned by grand Baroque monasteries paid for with Brazilian gold. I get off at Largo da Graça and head back down the hill, spending the rest of the day exploring all the places I've just passed. Lunch is a picnic on the walls of the Castelo (followed by a nap in its orchard-like garden). The sun and sky have a Mediterranean clarity, and yet the breeze, off the Atlantic, carries an open-ocean coolness. As afternoon stretches past 20:00, I head to the statue of Fernando Pessoa in the Chiado, the city's favoured meeting point. Friends arrive in dribs and drabs, and we eventually stroll down to the Miradouro Santa Catarina to watch river, sky and city turn rosy, then purple. There is still colour in the sky when, after 22:00, we sit down for beer and seafood at Trindade. Our midnight arrival at the Bairro Alto clubs is premature, but there's no wait for drinks. Tomorrow, I remind myself, I can sleep in.

CITY HIGHLIGHTS

London Eye | Go sky-high for a unique view of the capital.
Brick Lane | Shop in eclectic boutiques and enjoy a vindaloo in London's biggest selection of curry houses.
Natural History Museum | Dinosaurs, whales and all manner of creepy-crawlies are housed in one of London's most beautiful buildings.
River cruise | Drift along the Thames to Greenwich and enjoy a riverside view with an entertaining historical commentary.
Hampstead Heath | Be inspired by the countryside with a picnic and city views.

The Perfect Day in
LONDON

Former Londoner **Katja Gaskell** votes the city 'one of the most exciting and dynamic in the world'.

Providing I'm not suffering too much from Friday night my favourite day in London has to be Saturday and it always starts with a strong coffee at Monmouth Café at Borough Market, south of the river.

Once the caffeine has kicked in and the papers have been read it's time for a stroll around one of my favourite London markets (open Fridays and Saturdays), ideal for those with a passion for food. Speciality delis, organic butchers and row upon row of mouthwatering food stalls make it a colourful place to wander. With breakfast (or rather, brunch) over it's time for a bit of culture. London has a wealth of museums and galleries to choose from, but the one I like best for just ambling around is the Tate Modern. Easily one of Britain's most popular Millennium projects, the Tate Modern has been transformed from an empty power station into a powerhouse of modern art and there's always something weird and wonderful on display to capture my imagination. If I'm feeling particularly cultured I might hop on the Tate (Modern) to Tate (Britain) boat service that links new with old and stops at the London Eye along the way. It's more likely, however, that I'll choose to stretch my legs and stroll along the South Bank, which in summer months is one of the best ways to get a feel for all that London has to offer. In addition to the galleries, theatres and museums lined up along the river there are outdoor cafés, festivals and musicians to enjoy. Late afternoon and it must be time for a drink of some kind. If I'm feeling flush I'll head to Windows on the World on the top floor of the Hilton. You might not be able to see France from here, but the view of London's skyline is unparalleled and there's something wonderfully decadent about sipping on a cocktail as the sun goes down.

The Perfect Day in
LOS ANGELES

Los Angeles author **Sara Benson** will defend LA to the death against any silly Bay Area prejudices.

For an action-packed day in LA, I've got to rouse myself and get out of bed early.

I start off stuffing myself silly with sugary pancakes at the Griddle Cafe in West Hollywood, or have a power breakfast at the classic Polo Lounge inside the legendary Beverly Hills Hotel. Then I cruise east into the heart of Hollywood, paying my respects to the stars along the Walk of Fame and outside Grauman's Chinese Theater. I stop and snap a photo of the famous Hollywood sign inside the Babylon Court at glitzy Hollywood & Highland mall, then grab a fresh lemonade and french fries at punk Skooby's hot-dog stand. The afternoon is for browsing the unique boutiques and vintage shops in bohemian Los Feliz, at Silver Lake's Sunset Junction or along famous Melrose Ave. Cruising back west down Sunset Blvd, I can't resist detouring to the hilltop Getty Center for an infusion of arts and culture in a postmodernist architectural setting. Timing it just right, I arrive at Santa Monica Pier as the sun sinks into the Pacific Ocean while I take a breezy walk along the beach or a solar-powered Ferris-wheel ride. Then I grab dinner with friends on Santa Monica's eclectic Main St or at funky Venice Beach. After dark, we all line up for a comedy or live-music show on the Sunset Strip and afterwards groove at the Hollywood's Cahuenga Corridor dance clubs till the wee hours of the morning. Finally, we finish up at the Standard hotel's late-night lounge or maybe 24-hour Canter's Delicatessen, open since the 1930s in Mid-City's Fairfax District.

CITY HIGHLIGHTS

Wat Xieng Thong | The sweeping roof of the city's most famous temple is simply stunning.

Royal Palace and National Museum | Reach into the royal past with a browse through the king's former residence.

Pak Ou Caves | Take a boat up the Mekong to these dramatic caves, home to thousands of Buddha images placed here by pilgrims of old.

Night market | Shop till you drop at this lively street market on Th Sisangvong.

Kuang Si Waterfall | Immerse yourself in turquoise waters at beautiful jungle cascades.

The Perfect Day in
LUANG PRABANG

Multitalented *Southeast Asia on a Shoestring* author **Nick Ray** lives in nearby Cambodia.

It pays to break the habit of a lifetime and rise early in Luang Prabang.

At the crack of dawn the city's many temples open their doors and hundreds of monks spill onto the streets in search of alms. Locals line the streets and the sight is spectacular as the saffron robes disappear into the distance. After paying my respects with some instant noodles, I figure it is time for a steaming bowl of soup to set me up for the day. Nang Sengdao is the venue of choice, home to some of the best *foe* (rice noodles) in town. While things are still cool, I board a boat upriver to the Pak Ou Caves. The river trip is blindingly beautiful and the caves are

perfect to visit time and time again, as the various Buddha images gradually reveal themselves. Across the water is a cluster of local restaurants on stilts that offers the perfect view of Pak Ou over a fruit shake. Feeling hungry, it's time for a local lunch on the banks of the Mekong. Several places line the pavement along Th Khem Khong – all offer fresh Lao flavours at low prices. After a short siesta the late afternoon sees me wandering through the small streets and alleys of the historic temple district to Wat Xieng Thong. Sunset is a good time to capture this beautiful wat's charm. I might climb the hill of Phu Si for a dramatic view of town, but if the

clouds are coming in I wander down to the Apsara for a drink. The drink leads to dinner, as the fusion menu here is one of the best in town – owner Ivan is always experimenting with new recipes. Feeling fulfilled, I wander through the night market picking up some pieces here and there. Eventually and inevitably I end up at the Hive Bar, one of the coolest drinking dens in town.

A Buddhist monk contemplates the external world from a gilded doorway of Wat Xieng Thong. **John Banagan**

CITY HIGHLIGHTS

Museo del Prado | Wander among the Masters in one of the finest art galleries in the world.

Plaza Mayor | Take a seat and watch street musicians and a passing parade of Madrid life in this spectacular city square.

Nightlife | Dive into Europe's most dynamic after-dark city, especially in the streets of Malasaña, Chueca or Huertas.

Parque del Buen Retiro | Join all of Madrid in the city's green heart on a Sunday.

Palacio Real | Imagine yourself as royalty in this beautiful royal palace.

The Perfect Day in
MADRID

Inveterate traveller and writer **Anthony Ham** is a resident of Madrid.

I have a lazy start – Madrid is not a city that gets up early.

For breakfast I'd indulge in *chocolate con churros* (Spanish donuts with hot chocolate) at El Brilliante on Calle de Eloy Gonzalo before retiring to an outdoor table (in summer) around Plaza de Olavide to catch up on the latest news. I only make it as far as Café Comercial on Glorieta de Bilbao before diving headlong into the irresistible energy around the Puerta del Sol. Another pit stop is required by this stage – it's all an excuse, really, to enjoy one of Europe's finest café cultures – and for this I choose one of Madrid's charming plazas – Plaza Mayor, Plaza de la Paja or Plaza de Santa Ana are old favourites. At the latter, I enjoy an atmospheric lunch either in or overlooking the plaza before the heat (or cold) drives me indoors to one of Madrid's world-class art galleries – Museo del Prado, Centro de Arte Reina Sofia and Museo Thyssen-Bornemisza – or under the shade of a tree in the wonderful Parque del Buen Retiro. As sunset approaches and Madrid comes to life, I have a drink at Café del Real before watching the sun go down from Plaza de Oriente. Madrid nights are epic, but they don't begin until late. To ease into the night, I start with a late meal along Calle de Manuela Malasaña near the Glorieta de Bilbao – preferably La Musa, Nina or La Isla de Tesoro – followed by a *mojito* (rum, lime and mint cocktail) in Café Belén or one of the many small bars in Conde Duque. If I'm in for a late one – Madrid is at its best in the wee hours – I head to Huertas or Lavapiés and dance the night away.

The Perfect Day in
MANCHESTER

Etain O'Carroll lives and works in Oxford, and wrote for the *Britain* and *England* guidebooks.

Most Manchester mornings start off with a bleary head from the night before, and in the city that sets the standard for partying, it's best to take things gently in the morning.

For me this means a visit to at least one of the city's incredible museums. Housed in cutting-edge buildings worthy of a visit in their own right, the Lowry and the Imperial War Museum take art and a sombre history and turn them into compelling viewing. If I'm in town, it'll be the glass triangle of Urbis that gets my attention and brings home the truth about modern city living. Avoiding the chichi shops and boutiques of the city centre it's time for a wander around Castlefield, one of my favourite parts of town. A vestige of the city's industrial past and a haven of formidable red-brick warehouses, elegant market buildings, cast-iron relics, and crisscrossing viaducts, railway lines and canals, it's got the edgy chic of an industrial wasteland gentrified by loft-style living and a clutch of hip restaurants and bars. A few hours spent wandering here is always rewarded with some strange chance encounter and a glimpse of the city's shadowy underbelly. A few lazy drinks and a mellow meal on the canal bank later and I'm set for a climb up the vertiginous spiral staircase at the Godlee Observatory, a turn of the 20th century classic offering incredible views of the city and the skies. Suitably star-struck and kicked out just when the pubs are beginning to fill up, it seems a shame to go home so soon, so the only real decision to make is where to settle in for the first pint of the evening.

CITY HIGHLIGHTS

Djemaa el-Fna | One of the greatest spectacles on earth.
Souks | Experience the exciting, intimidating and absorbing world of the souks.
Riad Mehdi or La Maison Arabe Hammam | For the best pampering that money can buy.
Mamounia Gardens | The meticulously maintained gardens of the Mamounia are perfect for afternoon tea.
Dar Marjana and Dar Moha | An absolutely unforgettable dining experience equal to your wildest Arabian fantasy.

The Perfect Day in
MARRAKESH

Marrakesh fan **Paula Hardy** has written for six Lonely Planet guidebooks, including *Morocco*.

In Marrakesh everything happens in the evening – the day is merely a hot waiting room for the night's activities.

So mornings tend to be slow, a glass of freshly squeezed orange juice on the terrace of Cafe Argana or a *café au lait* in Gueliz with the morning's newspapers and then a lunch in Gueliz at the latest café (there's always somewhere new to try!). At the moment it's Kechmara with its cool, air-conditioned, whiter-than-white interior. Everyone congregates here so I always see familiar faces or bump into people I haven't seen for ages. The afternoon is dispensed with lolling around the pool at Les

Jardins de la Koutoubia. Then at 17:00 it's time for wicked indulgence at La Maison Arabe or one of the other fantastic *hammams* (bathhouses) around town. A vicious scrub down and then I lie prone while someone administers that French manicure I couldn't afford in London. Between 18:00 and 19:00 it's time for the souks. This is when everyone in town descends on them. It's noisy and exciting and I love the way you're just swept along with the huge body of humanity that fills the tiny alleys. In the square you can feel them limbering up for the evening, setting up their stalls. You can hear the drums before you reach the square – they seem to get

a hold of you and drag you towards the mesmerising scene. Rows of barbeques, men touting for business, naked bulbs strung across the square and smoke enveloping everything like some moody film set. It's great fun to sit at one of the benches and chow down on kebabs and spicy plates of Moroccan salad with friends. Then a cab to silly, stylish Comptoir or Jad Mahal where I have to affect lounging in style and compete (unsuccessfully) for attention with the spangly-suited belly dancers.

CITY HIGHLIGHTS
Rue Bebelons | Smooth yet genuine bar.
Fitzroy Gardens | Lush greenery right in the city's backyard.
Chinatown | For the Chinese food, of course.
Federation Square | For a unique perspective on Melbourne.
Victoria St, Richmond | For Vietnamese food and people-watching.

The Perfect Day in
MELBOURNE

Simon Sellars is a Melbourne-based writer/editor and one of the authors of *Bluelist*.

Melbourne's parks and gardens do the trick most of the year. And luckily the CBD is surrounded by choice examples.

The Fitzroy Gardens are popular with wedding parties – with English elms and colonial flowerbeds lining the paths, it's bliss, wedded or not. Despite the brides, grooms and preponderance of peach- and pink-coloured outfits, I still have the opportunity to hide from lovebirds and glory seekers, with trickling creeks and hidden walkways all about. I choose a nook and take the opportunity to read the newspaper in peace; after all these years, I'm still amazed that the city is just 10 minutes' walk

away – from here you can't see it and you can't hear it, so it doesn't exist if you don't want it to. Handy for flashers, admittedly, but also for solitude seekers; just pick your turf carefully. Sadly, there's not much in Melbourne's papers these days so I end up throwing the wretched tabloid away and make a snap decision to hit Chinatown for an early lunch. There are a lot of restaurants in this condensed neighbourhood and a lot of brazen touts; ignoring their bleating I just follow my nose and settle for sizzling Mongolian beef. I vacuum it down before reflecting on how unbelievably bone idle I suddenly feel. Alright, that does it: work can get

knotted for the day. I hit a bar, Rue Bebelons, just near the State Library, with Latino décor, laconic staff, a smart music policy and cheap spirits. I pull out a book, something by JG Ballard no doubt, sit at the bar with a scotch and a beer chaser, and watch the seething masses pass by the floor-length front windows. Only a few hours till dinner and the agony of being spoilt for choice (and of blowing yet another deadline) happens all over again.

CITY HIGHLIGHTS

National Anthropology Museum | Survey the remarkable remnants of the nation's ancient cultures.

Centro Histórico | Wander amid colonial and pre-colonial masterpieces in the city's historic core, declared a UNESCO World Heritage site.

Plaza Garibaldi | Get serenaded in this mariachi mecca, then taste tequila at the Tenampa cantina.

Coyoacán | Soak up the bohemian atmosphere of Diego and Frida's old 'hood.

Murals | Admire the legacy of the post-revolutionary muralists at the National Palace and other buildings.

The Perfect Day in
MEXICO CITY

Editor, writer and sometime ESL teacher **Daniel Schechter** lived nearly 10 years in Mexico City.

The day begins in Condesa, the bohemian enclave west of the city centre, where I meet a journalist friend at the Café Toscano, on Parque México, to discuss the baroque complexities of Mexican politics.

Later, we cut across the park, a delightful patch of palms and jacarandas, to our favourite taco joint, called Hola!, and fill up on squash blossoms and cactus leaves. This being Tuesday, I make for the weekly *tianguis* (indigenous market). The market extends for several blocks and I survey the artfully arranged hills of *poblano* peppers and mangos while listening to the vendors' spiels, then visit the prepared food section for *mixiotes* (spiced mutton steamed in maguey-leaf sacks). Thus fortified, I head for Bosque de Chapultepec, the city forest, and climb the hill to Chapultepec Castle, Emperor Maximilan's former residence, for a matchless view down Paseo de la Reforma. Next is La Ciudadela, the sprawling crafts market, to meet my wife who's there to purchase a set of coloured glass cocktail stirrers from Tlaquepaque. As it's lunch time, we head east to El Cuadrilatero, the wrestlers' café, and after greeting owner and former *lucha libre* (professional wrestling) champ Super Astro, we split half a gargantuan Torta Gladiador.

Continuing to Eje Central, I make my way up the vendor-clogged boulevard to the Art-Nouveau Palacio de Bellas Artes to catch the an exhibition, then barely make the old Jesuit College of San Ildefonso for a screening of Santo vs the Martian Invasion. Later I meet some wrestling enthusiast friends at the Arena Coliseo for live *lucha libre* action. Tonight's top bout: Shocker versus Tarzan Boy. Afterward, we walk to the lively Plaza Garibaldi (mariachi central), first stopping into the adjacent San Camilito market building for *pozole* (hearty broth brimming with pork and hominy kernels), then knock back a few tequilas at Tenampa cantina.

CITY HIGHLIGHTS

South Beach Art Deco | Kick off a wonderful walking tour at the Art-Deco Welcome Center and buy cool Deco mementos while you're at it.

South Beach | Rub elbows with shirtless posers, rollerblading scenesters and kooky locals – the backbone of the beach culture.

Coconut Grove to Coral Gables | Take a driving tour along Biscayne Bay and on through George Merrick's stylish neighbourhood.

Little Havana | Wander in and out of shops, galleries and cafés on Calle Ocho before the developers reduce the Latin neighbourhood to something unrecognisable.

Metromover | Ride the elevated tracks downtown at dusk to survey the lay of the land.

The Perfect Day in
MIAMI

Kim Grant is the author of the *Florida* guide and has been writing guidebooks since 1987.

Begin your morning with people-watching on Ocean Ave paired with a fresh omelette at the Front Porch Café in South Beach. Walk it off with a stroll through this fabled neighbourhood, being sure to include a hop along Lincoln Rd.

If there's a farmers market, pick up some avocados and papayas. If not, spend your time poring over cool clothes at any number of boutiques. Grab a shot of Cuban coffee from David's Café and then get ready to drink in some fresh air. Take a leisurely bike ride along the breezy paths of Key Biscayne. On the drive back to the mainland, meander through the lush roads of Coral Gables. Then hightail to the mid-beach Boardwalk for a sunset run. After showering, bring on the nightlife: listen to music while sipping a Design District cocktail, dip into an art gallery opening and duck into any one of the city's wonderful eateries. Soyka maybe? Or how about Nemo? Or Miss Yip?

In addition to colourful tropical libations at the Marlin or Raleigh hotels, a nightcap could come in many other forms. Take in an indie film at Miami Beach Cinematheque, an elegant moonlight stroll along South Beach or start club hopping at someplace that's so new I can't even write about it yet.

The Perfect Day in
MILAN

Best of Milan author **Terry Carter** declared his love for the city on buying his first Alfa Romeo at 21.

My top day is kick-started with an espresso at Zucca in Galleria at the Galleria Vittorio Emanuele II. I always find that a morning of art provides an inspiring start to the day, and never tire of visiting Da Vinci's magnificent The Last Supper.

The Pinacoteca de Brera is equally irresistible, with its wonderful Raphaels, Bellinis, and Caravaggios. Or if I'm in the mood for something more modern I'll head to the Padiglione d'Arte Contemporanea (PAC). Another favourite museum of mine is the wonderful Museo degli Strumenti Musicali, a must for musicians and music lovers. For lunch, I generally head straight to Trattoria Bagutta where I

can count on sincere service and excellent old-fashioned Milanese cuisine. Although I know I should probably have a siesta, it's hard to resist a visit to the roof of the Duomo; its views are all the more breathtaking after a few glasses of wine. If I eat three courses at lunch I'll take the stairs, and the lift if I stick to two. Lining up for tickets to an opera at the renovated La Scala is worth the wait, before heading down to the Naviglio Grande for a Milanese must – *aperitivo* hour. If I'm still hungry after grazing the snack tables at a couple of bars I'll grab a quick pizza at Officina 12, before racing back for the opera. I'll walk back to the hotel through

the Quadrilatero D'Oro when the streets are at their most atmospheric, the illuminated window displays looking their best at night. If I didn't have any luck getting opera tickets, then I'll save myself for a memorable meal at Cracco-Peck. If I'm up for more, I'll stroll down Via Torino to Porta Ticinese and join the locals for a nightcap among the atmospheric columns of San Lorenzo alle Colonne.

CITY HIGHLIGHTS

Old Port | Cobblestone streets twist and wind through a city frozen in time.

Gay Village | Experience an alternative nightlife that pulsates with the music.

Ave Duluth | Grab a bottle of wine and experience Mediterranean bistros the way the French do.

Marché Jean Talon | Let your eyes and nose devour a feast of cheeses, smoked meats and a kaleidoscopic display of fresh flowers.

Crescent St | Hit the dance floor in one of the street's many nightclubs.

The Perfect Day in
MONTREAL

Sarah Richards is a contributor to www.lonelyplanet.com.

The prospect of a *pain au chocolat* and steamy cappuccino on the terrasse of a Quartier Latin patisserie is reason enough to set my alarm clock. On a rainy day I like to bring along a Montreal Gazette to devour, in case the rain interferes with my favourite hobby of people-watching. If I'm feeling particularly bouncy, a hike up Mont Royal to Kondiaronk Lookout is a great way to expend all that caffeine, and burn those pastry calories.

On days when Mother Nature is in a good mood, I meet up with friends for a gourmet sandwich aside the waterfall in Cafe Santropol's back-yard jungle. But if a downpour threatens to ruin the alfresco ambience, we brave the fluorescent lights for a comforting bowl of noodles in Chinatown's Pho Bac.

Next I'll window shop my way along Ste Catherine to McGill station, bid farewell to downtown and metro over to the east end. A few hours are just enough to savour Marché Jean Talon, a sinful feast for the eyes and nose, and nearby Marché des Saveurs, where I can choose a bottle of wine for my dinner in Little Italy. If I'm feeling especially lucky after my Mediterranean feast, I'll hop in a cab going to Île Ste Hélène and throw whatever remains in my wallet into the slots at glitzy Casino de Montréal.

The futuristic architecture of the Casino de Montreal at Parc Jean-Drapeau. **Richard Cummins**

CITY HIGHLIGHTS

Elephanta Island | Easy to reach and riddled with temple caves and carvings, including a giant three-headed Shiva.

Chowpatty Beach | The best beach for walks and the city's famous snack – *bhelpuri*.

Chhatrapati Shivaji Maharaj Museum | Chock-full of Mughal miniatures, carvings and arcane weapons.

Food glorious food | Munch your way around India in the eateries of Fort and Colaba.

Shopping | Shopaholics should head to Colaba or Fort for trinkets and ethnic clothing, or the Mutton St market for antiques and bric-a-brac.

The Perfect Day in MUMBAI

Joe Bindloss has lost count of the Lonely Planet titles he's worked on, but *Best of Mumbai* is one.

Days in Mumbai start early, with coffee and a muffin at the nearest branch of Barista or with a plate of *idli* (steamed rice cakes) at one of Colaba's south Indian dining halls.

Then stroll along Colaba Causeway to watch the vendors setting up market stalls laden with T-shirts, incense, soapstone elephants, discount electronics and *faux* antiques. Take a ride in one of Mumbai's charming old taxis – modelled on 1950s Fiats – to the bizarre colonial fantasy that is Victoria Station, followed by a wander round the faded but still stately streets of the old British quarter. For the second half of the morning, I'd

be torn between visiting the splendid Chhatrapati Shivaji Maharaj Museum or a jaunt to Chowpatty Beach for a promenade on the sands and a plate of Mumbai's famous *bhelpuri* salad. Or I could have lunch at the phenomenally popular Cream Centre – assuming I can get a table. After lunch, I'd head back to Colaba for a boat ride to the famous Hindu cave temples on Elephanta Island (not before making sure anything that looked edible was hidden from the eyes of hungry monkeys). The tail end of the afternoon would be spent shopping for ethnic knick-knacks and Indian fashions on Dr DN Rd in Fort or Linking Rd in Bandra. A shower

and a change of clothes would be essential for dinner at Khyber, Mumbai's best eatery, styled after an Afghan palace and serving food fit for a Mughal emperor. Belly full, I'd drift back to Colaba for an ice-cold Kingfisher beer and a chat with interesting punters at the energetic Leopold Cafe. Suitably refreshed, there might still be time for a late showing of a Bollywood blockbuster at the swish Inox cinema at Nariman Point.

CITY HIGHLIGHTS

English Garden | Kick back, picnic or swim in Munich's leafy backyard.

Schloss Nymphenburg | Feast your eyes on the treasures of this royal summer residence.

Pinakothek Museums | Old Masters to Andy Warhol – this trio of museums provides the ultimate kick for art lovers.

Hirschgarten | Join locals for pretzels and beer, and watch the deer scampering about at this delightful beer garden.

Shop till you drop | Head to Maximilianstrasse for *haute couture* or Reichenbachstrasse for one-of-a-kind.

The Perfect Day in
MUNICH

German born and bred, **Andrea Schulte-Peevers** is the author of the *Munich & Bavaria* guide.

Die Toten Hosen, that forever-young German punk band, thrashes it out on my alarm-clock radio as I slowly peel back the lids of my encrusted eyeballs after a night on the razzle.

I hazily remember an evening with friends that started with sausage and beer under the chestnut trees of the rambling Augustiner beer garden and ended with a minty *mojito* among the beau monde at Bar Centrale. Time to restore balance to the brain with a hearty breakfast. I swing myself on my trusty old bike, dodging trams and traffic on my way to the Café am Beethovenplatz for a high-octane caffeine kick, buttery croissants and homemade

jams. Still not feeling particularly ambitious, I decide to spend the rest of the morning browsing around the small designer and vintage boutiques of the Gärtnerplatzviertel. From here it's off to the Viktualienmarkt, whose bonanza of gourmet foods, though pricey, never fails to impress. I pick up some cheese and bread and find a spot in the sun for an impromptu picnic and a people-watching session. A little culture is in order for the afternoon, so I pedal over to the Pinakothek der Moderne, an awesome showcase of modern and contemporary art. I feast my eyes on works by Klee, Kandinsky and de Kooning, but as usual I'm just as

awed by the building's boundary-pushing design that floods the galleries with soft natural light. My cell phone rings: it's Jenny asking me to join her for Blade Night, that great Munich summer tradition when thousands of inline skaters whiz along closed-off streets on Monday evenings. We meet up first at Riva to fortify ourselves on the best thin-crust pizza in town, then spend the next couple of hours racing each other to work it all off. Blade Night ends with a big street party but, for once, I decide to be a good girl and make it an early night.

Fans showing their colours at a soccer match in the packed Allianz-Arena, home to Bayern Munich. **Johannes Simon**

CITY HIGHLIGHTS

Mutrah Fish Market | Sizing up the opposition before signing up for a dive.

Mutrah Souk | Haggling avidly over gold bangles and frankincense – and leaving instead with a singing camel and a mosque clock.

Beautiful beaches | Losing half a chicken *shwarma* to a gull or a heron while sucking down the scenery.

Khor tour | Keeping up with the dolphins on a tour of Muscat's inlets.

Friday brunch | Indulging yourself at one of Muscat's elegant hotels and sleeping through the guilt under a date palm.

The Perfect Day in
MUSCAT

The Sultanate of Oman has been writer **Jenny Walker**'s home for the past seven years.

I'd have to begin my day early, because days in Muscat start early.

The ministry buildings open at 07:30, the banks at 08:30, the shopping is over by 13:00 and the citizens of Muscat are all home again by 15:00, enjoying that great Middle Eastern tradition: the afternoon nap. If I'm getting up early, then I may as well take consolation from the fishermen, who were up so early that they haven't been to bed yet. I'll watch them unload their catch of yellow-finned tuna, sardines and squid, together with a dream sequence of sharp-nosed, slim-bodied and top-eyed curiosities of the deep at the Fish Market in Mutrah. A stroll along Mutrah's famous corniche, beneath the balconied windows of old merchant houses, should blow away the last of the cobwebs, or at least the smell of the fish market. Containers from Korea, the odd boatload of goats from Iran, the wondrous cargo of the modern era – a little bit of everything turns up in Mutrah's aged souk. This is where I head for a breakfast of mango-and-pomegranate juice and watch the dramas of courting and haggling, mock tempers and handshakes shared by stock exchanges the world over. Armed with gold, home-grown frankincense and myrrh from the souk, I may as well pop into the Bait az-Zubair Museum and see how these precious commodities are woven into the cultural experience of the country. It'll also remind me why nearby Muscat Harbour was worth the brooding protection of two Portuguese Forts. The modern palace of the Sultan signals the 20th-century Renaissance of this great country, which has adapted so well to the modern age without losing its respect for the past. Late lunch at Al-Bustan Palace Hotel and a snooze on its beautiful beach wraps up the afternoon in extravagant local style before I head over the hill to Bandar Jissah for a sunset cruise and fine dining in Muscat's very own Shangri-la.

Muscat's whitewashed buildings stand out among the stark desert hills. **Christine Osborne**

CITY HIGHLIGHTS

Brooklyn Bridge | Walk beneath the fabled 19th-century gothic arches (walking from Brooklyn means better views).

Bryant Park | Read under the trees amid midtown's towering buildings.

Chelsea galleries | Gallery-hopping the free cutting-edge exhibits on Saturday is as New York as the Yankees.

Brunch | Have a meal at one of the serious-about-breakfast eateries all over town or celebrate the soul-saving Bloody Mary.

Central Park | It's big and beautiful and a serious testament to forward thinking.

The Perfect Day in
NEW YORK CITY

Robert Reid first moved to NYC in 1992, fuelled by a surprise ticket for a Keith Richards show.

I've lived in New York City for over 10 years, but it took Brooklyn for me, a transplanted Okie, to finally call New York home.

Unsurprisingly, my best day begins with brunch in Brooklyn at a classic American diner, with egg cream drinks and cheeeap eggs and pancakes. Tom's Restaurant in Prospect Heights, at 782 Washington Ave, may just be the cheeriest eatery north of the Mason Dixie line (staff hand out coffee, orange slices and cookies to those in line). Another starting spot, Carroll Gardens' Smith St is lined with breakfast spots, most with a French tinge. Tuba-packing bands play merrily by the sidewalk tables. After brunch, I might wander to Brooklyn Heights, peek at furniture shops or used bookshops on Montague St, then walk along the promenade overlooking the East River (and Manhattan). If I've dallied long enough, I'd grab a hot pie at Grimaldi's (19 Old Fulton St) – a classic brick-oven pizzeria under Brooklyn Bridge – then stroll over the bridge to Manhattan. I'd then subway up to Chelsea for a peek at some of the dozens of free galleries. During the week, I might venture up to Midtown among some of the city's best street vendors for a grab-and-go lunch to eat at Bryant Park amid the sea of skyscrapers. Miriam's serves kosher falafel from the corner of Sixth Ave and W 46th St. Mr M insists that first timers sample the falafel before making a decision: 'All the best falafel places do this,' he says. Before heading back to Brooklyn, I might stop for some sake at Decibel, at 240 E Ninth St, in the East Village – a subterranean, timeless rah-rah Japanese place with wood stools and delicious snacks.

A boy practising karate kicks in the school yard. Eric L Wheater

CITY HIGHLIGHTS

Parque Natural Metropolitano | Get that steamy rainforest feeling and panoramic vistas just minutes from downtown.

Panama Canal | Have a picnic beholding this unparalleled engineering feat.

Dinner and dancing | Try the 12-course feast at Manolo Caracol, then work it off at the Calle Uruguay clubs.

Casco Viejo | Explore the hidden pockets of this seedy but funky colonial core.

Calzada de Amador | Cycle down 'lover's lane' to Isla Amador and enjoy vino and views at The Wine Bar.

The Perfect Day in
PANAMA CITY

Conner Gorry spent a year camping, backpacking and chicken bussing around Central America.

Taking full advantage of Panama's laid-back tropical pace, I'm sleeping in today, followed by a leisurely breakfast made by yours truly – there are so many good accommodation options with kitchen facilities here, I wouldn't stay somewhere I couldn't cook. The sun is getting high, so I pack up my picnic lunch of hard boiled quail eggs, olives, a couple of hard cheeses and some crappy bread (Panama has terrific food, but is severely bread challenged) and head to the street to flag a cab to Parque Natural Metropolitano.

This dense forest with moderate trails and a couple of lookout points provides deep detox from the exhaust and car alarms, loco 'red devil' buses and trilling mobile phones of the city. I consider going for a ride at the stables near the park entrance, but don't have the giddy up and go today to manage a horse – a walk in the park is about my speed. I know the trails well, but flowers have bloomed and the morpho butterflies are out in force, making it all seem new. I ascend the second lookout (better than the first and more pleasant for a picnic) and dine alone, looking out at the canal. That's where I'm headed next, to meet some friends for sunset cocktails at the restaurant perched over the Miraflores Locks. We've all seen it before, but the spectacle of those giant ships passing through combines with the awkward English and melodic Spanish narration to make it memorable every time. So too, is the 12-course meal at Manolo Caracol, where we keep going back as much for the sublime food as for the entertaining attentions of Manolo himself. By now, a midnight swim is in my sights...if I'm not yet a hazard to myself or others.

Champs-Élysées | Crowded, boisterous and a bit daggy, Paris' most famous avenue is best seen from the top of the Arc de Triomphe.

Eiffel Tower | More Parisian than Paris itself, the Tour Eiffel is most beautiful viewed looking up from its base.

Le Louvre | The world's richest art depository contains some of its favourite art.

Montmartre | The Paris of story, song and myth never really existed – but it's still fun.

Notre Dame | Visit the world's most awesome cathedral for both the sacred (rose windows) and the profane (tourist hordes).

The Perfect Day in
PARIS

Paris and *France* author **Steve Fallon** lives in London and travels to Paris as often as he can.

After a tiptop Paris night, a tiptoe Paris day might be in order, but let's (unreasonably) assume that I wake up bright-eyed and bushy-tailed in my friend's *belle époque* apartment near Place de la République on a Sunday morning.

To market, to market – in this case my favourite, Marché Bastille, to stock up on anchovy fillets, *trompettes de la mort* (a type of mushroom) and other 'essentials'. Afterwards, I'll wend my way through medieval Marais, stopping for a *grand crème* (coffee with cream) and a *pain au chocolat* (chocolate croissant) at Ma Bourgogne in the scrumptious Place des Vosges. The landmark bridge Pont de Sully leads to my favourite island, Île St-Louis, but once I reach the Île de la Cité, I'll eschew Notre Dame in favour of the smaller, more delicate Ste-Chapelle. Before lunch (somewhere on the Rue Montorgueil market street) I'll window-shop at the boutiques of Rue Étienne Marcel or have another look at the antique clothes for sale in the Galerie de Montpensier (it's Sunday!). Though close, the Louvre is just too daunting for a postprandial visit; instead I'll rent a bike from Fat Tire Bike Tours and play chicken with the traffic in the middle of Place de l'Étoile, where motorists entering the roundabout have right of way. If I feel culturally peckish, I'll make my way to the Musée Auguste Rodin and have a kip under the sculptor's sublime The Thinker. As far as I'm concerned, any corner café works for an *apéro* (sundowner), but since I'm having dinner at Juan et Juanita in Ménilmontant, I head for L'Autre Café; they've just got to have a bottle of Pastis 51 with my name on it.

The Perfect Day in
PHILADELPHIA

John Spelman's work for Lonely Planet includes *Philadelphia & the Pennsylvania Dutch Country.*

It's Tuesday. Bike in hand, I buy some fruit at the Italian Market and head over to the Last Drop on Antique Row to read the paper and drink some coffee. After a couple of hours I depart, admiring Rittenhouse Square en route to the Philadelphia Museum of Art, where I briefly consider a run up the steps before deciding that I'd rather not be a cliché. Getting my fill of Duchamp and furniture, I walk out the back of the museum and survey the Schuylkill River, Boat House Row and the ancient Fairmount Water Works.

Now feeling peckish, I ride to nearby Rose Tattoo Cafe to eat mushroom soup in a greenhouse. This accomplished, it's time to visit Old City, where I lock up the bike, grab another cup of coffee and wander around pastoral Independence National Historical Park. When nobody's looking, I glance affectionately at Carpenter's Hall. I then buy a bottle of wine and head to Djanjo or Tre Scalini, where I meet a friend for one of Philly's better BYO meals. Now it's time to ride to the Standard Tap in Northern Liberties for an evening of beer, unless there's an irresistible rock show at the North Star or in the basement of the First Unitarian Church. I finish the day around 03:00 at the Center City Pretzel Co in South Philly, where I shove a hot one down my oesophagus before staggering home.

The Perfect Day in
PHNOM PENH

Based in Phnom Penh, **Andrew Burke** is a journalist, photographer and author of *Laos*.

Assuming I'm not sleeping off a late night, Phnom Penh is most charming during an early-morning stroll from my house to the river and north along its banks.

The promenade will be packed later on, but at this time of day I can stop under a tree and watch the fishermen work their nets and ferries crab their way across the current. Coffee and a croissant in one of the riverfront cafés is a natural progression and allows for great people-watching – cyclos, motos, vendors and occasional beggars all add to the mix. Phnom Penh's markets are among the most memorable aspects of the city and as I wander towards home I stop in the colourful Psar Kandal to haggle for mangoes or rambutans. The somewhat faded Art-Deco masterpiece that is Psar Thmei draws my friends and me for lunch among the steamy soup stalls. Phnom Penh has a growing art scene and I drop into at least one of the galleries, such as Popil PhotoGallery, which has regular exhibitions by local and international photographers. While the mornings are undoubtedly charming, the afternoons and evenings in Phnom Penh are a more liquid brand of entertainment. A top day sees me and a few friends hire a river boat for a two-hour cruise along the Tonle Sap and up the Mekong River.

The whole process is so Phnom Penh – just bowl up to the river, find a boat, negotiate a price and off you go. Having been to the Hotel Le Royal for happy-hour cocktails more times than I can remember, I get the boat to drop us at Snow's Place, a ramshackle wooden bar full of kitsch. Dinner at Cantina is possibly the best Mexican food in Indochina, and drinks at Rubies is a great way to finish off the night.

An ancient apsara dance being performed by the National Ballet in the Royal Palace Pagoda. **John Banagan**

CITY HIGHLIGHTS

Burma Banks | Dive one of Southeast Asia's premier dive sites – pristine and fabulously colourful.

Hollow Islands | Paddle a kayak through a subterranean passage and into this timeless and mysterious world.

Elephant ride | Take the pachyderm express through the fragrant mountain paths of Phuket's lush, jungle-clad interior.

Vegetarian Festival | Experience Phuket town's wild and bizarre food festival, on from late September to early October.

Nightlife | Sample hedonistic and carefree after-hours Phuket at one of Patong's countless pubs, bars or discos.

The Perfect Day in
PHUKET

Bangkok resident **Steven Martin** has been living and travelling in Southeast Asia since 1981.

There is nothing like having a wide and white stretch of tropical beach all to oneself, and in Phuket dawn is the best time to experience this joy.

Surf and the morning dew will have obscured the footprints of the previous day, and the crisp air will have only a hint of the balminess that comes with the rising sun. This is also the best time to tan naturally without burning, so enjoy a couple of hours 'sleeping in' on the beach, and then creep back to the hotel just in time for

a leisurely breakfast of papaya, pineapple and perhaps a mango or two. Then a drive up over the mountains and through the jungle in a *tuk-tuk* (open-air three-wheeled taxi) – the best way to sample the exotic sights and scents of the pristine Southeast Asian rainforest. Take a trip to the town of Phuket, the provincial capital, the vestiges of whose history as a crossroads of trade and culture can be seen in the charming and newly restored architecture.

After a spicy lunch of local Muslim curry eaten with crispy roti bread, head back to the hotel for an unhurried siesta, preferably upon a breezy veranda overlooking the ocean. After waking refreshed, it's time for a quick dip in the ocean to dispel any lingering drowsiness. Then it's time to go on the hunt for an appropriate seafood dish and a local beer, to fortify oneself for the nightlife that commences with a bang to match the surprisingly abrupt tropical dusk.

Motor scooters zip fully loaded in and out of Phuket's busy traffic. **Paul Beinssen**

CITY HIGHLIGHTS

Phewa Tal | Explore this lake by boat or kayak, or walk around its forested shore.

Old Pokhara | Lose yourself in an intriguing tangle of narrow streets, Newari houses and ancient temples.

World Peace Pagoda | With the Annapurna massif mirrored in the placid waters of the *tal*, this is arguably Pokhara's finest viewpoint.

International Mountain Museum | See the faces and equipment behind the first ascents of the world's highest peaks.

Dinner | Eat at some of the best restaurants in Nepal.

The Perfect Day in
POKHARA

Travel and food writer **Joe Bindloss** rates Nepal near the top in his list of favourite destinations.

The perfect day in Pokhara starts at first light, with a dawn boat-ride across the mist-shrouded lake to the Tewa Resort to begin the trek up to the World Peace Pagoda.

The trick is to reach the pagoda just as the morning sun lights up the whole panorama of Himalayan peaks, the perfect time for mountain photography. Several rustic cafés by the pagoda offer simple breakfasts and sweet Nepali tea, but I might stroll down the other side of the ridge to Kalimati and pick up a local bus back to town for coffee and a cinnamon bun at a bakery in Lakeside. The rest of the morning would be set aside for reading or planning a trek with a map of the Annapurna Conservation Area. For lunch Koto would be my top choice – the Japanese food is flawless. In the afternoon I'd rent a motorcycle and buzz into the old part of town to explore the winding alleys and Newari temples, moving on to the Seti Gorge viewpoint and Gurkha Museum on my way north to the Bat Cave. After wriggling through the damp and atmospheric exit tunnel, I'd return to the main road and take the winding mountain track to Sarangkot. It's a hairy, bumpy ride, but I'd be rewarded at the top with one of the best mountain views in the world – and that's no exaggeration. After being wowed by the sunset light show, I'd head down to Lakeside for a giant slab steak at the New Everest Steak House and a tankard of *tongba* (warm millet beer) at Lhasa Tibetan Restaurant. To finish the day, I'd drop the bike off at the hotel and join the noisy crowd in Club Amsterdam or the Busy Bee Café. Now, how does that Lou Reed song go again…?

A local man paddles through the dawn mist hovering over a lake. **Christian Aslund**

CITY HIGHLIGHTS

Powell's Books | Get lost in the world's largest independent bookshop, which takes up a full city block.

Forest Park | At 5000 acres (2000ha), the largest urban park in America is full of wonderful woodsy trails.

Saturday market | A Portland institution boasting creative and unique local crafts.

Portland's cool, quirky **Neighbourhoods** | From the Pearl District to Hawthorne Blvd, Alberta St and Mississippi Ave.

Pub theatres | Head to the Laurelhurst or the Bagdad, the Clinton or the Kennedy School (and so on). Order pizza and beer and enjoy the movie!

The Perfect Day in
PORTLAND

Sandra Bao has been an itinerant traveller since she first left her native Argentina at the age of eight.

Get up on a gloriously sunny August day (summer is when Portland is at her best). Hop on my bike and pedal west towards downtown, stopping at the Saturday Market just under the Burnside Bridge.

Buy a cool duct tape wallet, then go a few blocks up to Powell's Books, where I meet my friend Jami. We wander for a bit before heading over to the Pearl for lunch at Pho Van. After going our separate ways I bike up NW Thurman to Forest Park, where I ride the excellent Leif Erikson trail 8km (5mi) before turning back (it's a full 21km/13mi long!). Zoom downhill all the way to the flats, then turn left and slowly pedal through NW 23rd (or 'trendy-third'), checking out all the smart boutiques and cafés, along with the yuppies they attract. Ride back home, and garden for the rest of the afternoon – after all, Portlanders love their lush gardens! Later, when it's dark, grab hubby, Ben, and drive our Prius (Pdx's most popular and politically correct car) to the Kennedy School to meet Mark and Katie for some pub grub, a movie (in the old gymnasium) and a dip in the soaking pool – all in all, a quintessentially Portland experience.

Old piles in the Willamette River echo the buildings of the Portland skyline. **Richard Cummins**

Prague Castle | Spend the day exploring the city's undisputed historical jewel.

Jewish Museum | Discover the synagogues of Prague's fascinating former Jewish ghetto.

Centre for Modern & Contemporary Art | Cast an eye over this vast art collection.

Charles University Botanic Garden | Escape the crowds and relax among the trees and exotic flora.

Malá Strana | Wander the picturesque cobbled lanes of the lovely 'Lesser Quarter'.

The Perfect Day in
PRAGUE

One outcome of **Richard Watkins'** ongoing captivation with Prague was the *Best of Prague* guide.

A day in Prague usually involves a lot of walking, so I like to start with a quick caffeine dose; one of my favourite spots is the friendly Bakeshop Praha.

It does some very tasty muffins, and the English newspapers it provides are a bonus too. After that, I take a leisurely wander down to Old Town Square. Despite the heavy commercialisation, this is still a breathtaking sight, picture-postcard perfect from almost every angle. I walk along to nearby Týn Court for a browse round its shops, and then head to a gallery, either the House at the Golden Ring, with its typically surreal Czech artworks, or the new Museum of Czech

Cubism, which occupies Prague's most important cubist building, the House of the Black Madonna. Prague is the only place in the world where you'll find cubist architecture, and the angular style clearly appealed to the inventive, off-the-wall nature of the Czech people – unique cubist coffee sets, sofas and bookcases are also displayed here. I love the clean lines and geometric patterns of it all. After the crush of the Old Town I crave some greenery and open spaces, so I go north and cross the river to the peaceful Letná Gardens, and refresh myself with a couple of glasses of some of Prague's cheapest beer at the informal alfresco

bar. The views over the city from up here are magical. I'll probably be pretty hungry by now, so I'll have lunch at the excellent Brasserie Ullman in the park before heading back to the Old Town. A walk down the riverbank will clear my head and in the evening I'll head over to Vinohrady for dinner, or, if I'm in the mood for a bit of culture, I'll go along to a concert at the magnificent Rudolfinum, enjoying a glass of Bohemian champagne during interval.

CITY HIGHLIGHTS
Zona Romántica | Stroll down the cobbled streets past the red-roof-tiled buildings of Puerto Vallarta's ambient old town.
Yelapa | Take a water taxi to this remote beach, accessible only by boat.
Activities | Wear yourself out scuba-diving, fishing, eating, cruising or shopping.
Nightlife | Get wild and party down with the crowds at one of Vallarta's many hot spots.
Day trips | Venture out on a day trip north to Bucerías and Punta Mita, or south to loads of great beaches.

The Perfect Day in
PUERTO VALLARTA

Mexico contributor **Michael Read** has also worked as a graphic designer and exhibitions curator.

I roll out of bed early (09:00 is considered early in Vallarta) and slip down to my favourite café in the Zona Romántica for a strong coffee sweetened with an immoderate amount of Kahlua.

While many visitors prefer the pleasures of town, with its effervescent restaurant scene and endless shopping opportunities, my personal proclivities point me into the surrounding hills for hiking, mountain biking or horse riding, or, better yet, to a remote beach where I can ponder the horizon for an hour or three. On this particular day, the latter option wins out. I head to the pier at Playa de Los Muertos and hop on a

panga (water taxi) headed to Quimixto, 30 minutes away by sea. On arriving, and after an economical lunch of *pulpo* (octopus), I park myself under a *palapa* (thatched shelter) and gaze out to sea. Before long the horizon starts to bore me. A boy approaches to tell me of an inland 10m (33ft) waterfall and of the horse he has chosen to take me there, but I opt to make the easy half-hour hike on my own steam. On the way I spy a metre-long iguana passing stealthily through the branches of a rubber tree. Back in Vallarta, eminently satisfied with my adventure, I splurge on a well-priced massage before sauntering back to my room for a siesta. On rising,

I head to the Malecón for a sunset stroll, considering along the way which nightspot I'll choose to kick off the evening.

CITY HIGHLIGHTS

Skyline Gondola | Take a slow-moving trip to dizzying heights with fantastic views of Queenstown, the lake and the mountains.

Queenstown Gardens | Relax in this lush and peaceful setting, just footsteps from downtown.

Jetboating | Hop on a high-speed ride through the rocky canyons, with lots of 360° spins.

Bungy jumping | Dive off the historic Kawarau Bridge, the world's first commercial bungy site

Williams Cottage | Combine a little history with great shopping and coffee.

The Perfect Day in
QUEENSTOWN

At 18, **Korina Miller** left home with her backpack and she has been roaming the world ever since.

As many in Queenstown do, I get a late start. Breakfast at the Vudu Café is a must.

I slide into a booth with my giant bowl of latte and stack of blackberry pancakes and watch the mid-morning shoppers stroll down Beach St. I then head down to the harbour and along to Queenstown Gardens. Wandering along these lush pathways is a great way to start the day; not only do you get excellent views of the lake, surrounding mountains and the historic TSS *Earnslaw* chugging across the water, you also experience that excellent Kiwi openness with joggers, walkers and families all saying g'day. I find a bench and park myself down with a book for a while and then continue my loop of the grounds. When I return to Marine Parade, I realise it must be time for another coffee (it's just so good in NZ!) and pop into Vesta, a museum-cum-shop-cum-café where I can flick through design magazines and buy myself a cool pressie or two. I then wander back through town, having no trouble picking out the wired tourists who've been recently initiated into Queenstown's adrenaline hype via a jump from a bridge, a plane or a mountainside. I opt for a more relaxed trip and hop on a gondola carriage to the top of Bob's Peak. Once there I can't resist a few trips on the luge, racing through tunnels and along jack-knifed bends. I stay on the hilltop for incredible sunset views and then ride back down the gondola and head home to listen to George 93.6FM and recharge my batteries for dinner. If I'm feeling especially flush I meet friends at the very exclusive, very suave Bunker. If it's a jeans-and-T-shirt night I go to Winnie's for pizza and beer. Either way I stroll home along the lake, where the moon is reflected flawlessly on the water. Good as gold.

CITY HIGHLIGHTS

Ipanema Beach | Spend the day sunbaking and people-watching at Posto Nove.

Lapa | Catch the city's best live-music scene any weekend night in this samba-charged neighbourhood.

Sugar Loaf Mountain | Gaze out over the *cidade maravilhosa* (marvelous city).

Santa Teresa | Wander through the bohemian neighbourhood and stop for a bite in a colourful restaurant.

Corcovado | Ride the cog train up for stunning views beneath the open-armed Christ the Redeemer statue.

The Perfect Day in
RIO DE JANEIRO

Regis St Louis, author of the *Rio de Janeiro* guide, lists the city as one of his great loves.

Begin the day in Ipanema at the neighbourhood juice stand (Polis Sucos is a current favourite) with a glass of fresh *açai*, (made from a velvety vitamin-rich Amazonian berry).

Assuming the sky is clear, I head to Ipanema beach for a bit of a walk along the shore and perhaps a dip in the ocean. As lunch nears, I find my way to Leblon where I stroll the tree-lined streets, visiting a few boutiques and bookshops before having lunch at Sushi Leblon or one of the other choice spots on Rua Dias Ferreira (where nearly a dozen restaurants jockey for attention). As afternoon nears, I catch a taxi up to the bohemian

hilltop enclave of Santa Teresa, Rio's loveliest neighbourhood. There I wander the old streets, passing colourful, 19th-century mansions and taking in sweeping views over the city centre. If I'm lucky I'll bump into a friend in the neighbourhood and grab a drink or a light meal at one of Santa Teresa's atmospheric restaurants. Afterwards, it's time to reconnect with Rio's intoxicating music scene. I'll head down the hill to Lapa, a rugged neighbourhood of old samba clubs, venerable bars and outdoor drinking spots, any of which hosts outstanding live music. Tonight I'll try Democraticus, which

is always a great scene. Afterwards, I'll head back to Ipanema and call it a night, or perhaps rally a bit of energy and have a nightcap in Leblon at Melt or Bar D'Hotel.

CITY HIGHLIGHTS

Waiotapu | Be fascinated by swirling kaleidoscopes of mineral-rich water at the Champagne Pool.

Maori performance | Check out a *haka* before chowing down at a traditional *hangi* at the Mitai or Tamaki Maori Villages.

Mokoia Island | Take a lake cruise out to this sacred island.

Ohinemutu | This sweet village is a fusion of Christian and Maori traditions.

Tutanekai St | This famous street boasts some great eateries and bars.

The Perfect Day in
ROTORUA

George Dunford is a freelance web producer/ writer/editor/writing teacher/information leafblower.

Waking up to aroma of a rich sulphur smell makes me think this town could have been called Fartopolis, but it is actually due to the rich volcanic activity in the region.

To cover the smell a little I'll grab a coffee on Tutanekai St and walk up to Kuirau Park to watch the early-morning steaming of volcanic vents and mud pools bubbling. Then it's time for a dip so I'll grab some togs for a trip to the Blue Baths where I can relax in a traditional bathhouse.

Soaking until my stomach rumbles, I'll head over to Fat Dog Café for a meal that has defeated chubbier canines. Next is a wander across to Ohinemutu to see a very Maori-looking Jesus walking on water, which gets me thinking that I should take on the waves with the help of the *Lakeland Queen* paddle steamer. The cruise out to Mokoia Island is usually peaceful and you can expect an entertaining commentary from the captain. Once back in

town, it's time for dinner at the Pig & Whistle microbrewery. Depending on how exhausted I'm feeling I might head out for a Maori performance at Mitai Maori village or just stay at the pub for a cleansing pint of Swine Lager, the Pig & Whistle's microbrewed beer.

The Perfect Day in
SAN DIEGO

Susan Derby is a freelance writer now living a sunlit, sunscreen-slathered life in California.

With that relentless sunshine streaming in through the blinds, a day in San Diego is one that tends to start early.

If I'm in Pacific Beach, I put on my shades and join the fitness fiends on the boardwalk; I may even finally try out my new rollerblades (if I can just figure out how to brake...). Afterwards, I head down Garnet for a *chai* at a great café, Zanzibar – and I snatch one of its shockingly big cupcakes for later. Then, I head to Balboa Park where I picnic on grassy expanses under shaded groves. Of course, this happens in between visits to the San Diego Museum of Man, the San Diego Museum of Art and the botanic gardens. On a less ambitious day,

I'd be just as happy to come here with a fat book – the park is such a refreshing place for lingering, napping or just people-watching. Afterwards, I head to the nearby Hillcrest to browse cool vintage shops and used bookshops. Then, it's over to Ocean Beach for a sunset stroll. There are plenty of mellow stretches here, which I like, and if I need a little adrenaline jolt afterwards, Belmont Park's historic Giant Dipper roller coaster is nearby. Come dinner time, thoughts of Little Italy cast a *marinara*-infused spell. On a sidewalk-patio table at Buon Appetito, I order the *cioppino* (fish stew) – with a glass of white wine, it should be simply

perfetto. If I don't feel up to a few hours of shaking it up and sweating it out at Hillcrest's Brass Rail (from disco revival to hip hop!), I amble down to the inebriated Gaslamp Quarter and dip into one of the many bars for a cocktail and, if I'm lucky, some decent music. Finally, Cafe Bassam (open till 02:00) is the spot for a few swigs of chamomile tea (with 140 tea varietals on offer); this time, I'll pass on the cigar.

The Perfect Day in
SAN FRANCISCO

John Vlahides lives in San Francisco and is the author of *Coastal California*, among other guides.

Whenever friends visit, I build a walking-tour itinerary for them around four elements: hills, neighbourhoods, views and food – the four things that most define San Francisco.

Meet in the Financial District at the Ferry Building for coffee overlooking the glittering blue bay. Wander the food stalls and pick up Acme bread, Cowgirl Creamery cheese and farm-fresh local fruit to munch along the way. Ride the California St cable car, the line few tourists take because they don't know where it goes. Look back as you ascend Nob Hill for super-cool Bay Bridge views. At the terminus, walk one block north up Van Ness Ave to Sacramento St and

turn left (west). Amble past lovely Lafayette Park, where you can ascend the hill and see the cityscape. Turn right (north) on Fillmore St, the shopping street for Pacific Height's skirt-and-sweater matrons. At Broadway, ooh and aah over the mesmerising bay vistas and the mansions clinging to the hillsides, then descend the super-steep 18% grade, through Cow Hollow, into the Marina. At the bay, turn right (east) and walk along the water, in full view of Alcatraz, the kite-flyers at Marina Green and the bobbing sailboat masts of the small-craft harbour. Follow the footpath to Fort Mason and Aquatic Park, then amble out onto the pier. Bypass Fisherman's

Wharf for Columbus Ave and North Beach, the 'hood made famous by the Beats. Stop for meatball sandwiches at Mario's Bohemian Cigar Store, followed by espresso at Caffe Trieste. Climb Telegraph Hill to Coit Tower, check out the WPA murals, then descend 28 stories down the rickety wooden Filbert St steps to the Embarcadero waterfront and back to the Ferry Building. After a nap, meet for cocktails at Cafe Flore, then a movie at the fabulous 1920s-vintage Castro Theatre, followed by dinner at Chow on Church St, the best cheap eats in the 'hood. Then off to the Mission to see bands and shoot pool at the Elbo Room, or to swill cocktails on Valencia St.

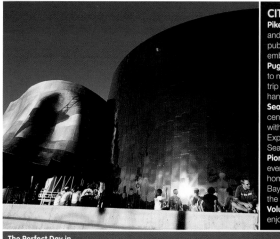

CITY HIGHLIGHTS

Pike Place Market | Cozy and rowdy, Seattle's finest public market is an excellent emblem for the city.

Puget Sound Ferry | It's hard to match the beauty of a day trip through America's most handsome islands.

Seattle Center | A cultural centre that actually works, with theatre, museums, the Experience Music Project and Seattle's Space Needle.

Pioneer Sq | You'll find everything from Safeco Field, home of the Mariners, to Elliott Bay Book Company, home of the world's best titles.

Volunteer Park | Relax and enjoy the Asian art museum.

The Perfect Day in
SEATTLE

Los Angeles-based **Andrew Bender** is living every MBA's dream: travelling and writing about it.

Clean, green, techie and serene, Seattle is a lower-key, less gritty version of San Francisco; in other words an ideal destination.

Don your hat and raingear, forget the umbrella (a sure sign of a visitor) and start the day at a coffee house. There's one on every block, or – if you dare – the original Starbucks. The heart of the action awaits at the Pike Place Market, eight warren-like blocks of shopping, browsing and snacking where getting a little disoriented is part of the fun. At Seattle Center, the enormous urban park dating back to the 1962 World's Fair, the Experience Music Project (EMP to its friends) is a must-visit to learn the story behind The Kingsmen's 'Louie, Louie' and Jimi Hendrix's 'Star Spangled Banner', The Presidents of the USA's 'Lump' and Nirvana's 'Smells Like Teen Spirit'. You can even test out your own skills on specially modified studio equipment. If you can, take a boat ride on the harbour as the afternoon light bathes the city in sun – or doesn't; it's still a gorgeous view. Then head in for a stroll as the lights come up on handsome, historic Pioneer Square. There are plenty of dining and nightlife options here, but my money is on the up-and-coming Belltown neighbourhood where Cyclops is always hip and Marjorie's creates innovative fusion cuisine in a bohemian setting. After dinner, Crocodile Cafe is something of a temple. It's where the grunge scene got its start, and so I'll leave you here to contemplate Nirvana.

CITY HIGHLIGHTS

Soak yourself | Cleanse the body and refresh the soul in the soothing hot and cold tubs of a public bath.

Eat dog meat | Try this Korean dish, widely regarded as stamina food.

Update your wardrobe | Indulge in a tailor-made suit or pair of handmade shoes from Itaewon's haberdashers and cobblers.

Party all night | Hit the dance clubs around Hongik University, where the action doesn't stop until you leave.

Experiment | Experience the latest food fad – melding green tea and desserts in Myeong Dong's teashops.

The Perfect Day in
SEOUL

Rob Whyte lives in Busan and dreams of lands where a round of golf doesn't cost US$200.

A good outing in Seoul involves eating, drinking and getting naked with the locals. The day begins with a spicy cold noodle breakfast in Namdaemun market and a surround sound encounter with Korea's eating customs.

The shopkeeper in front of me keeps barking, 'Oh so seyo' (welcome) and 'Kuksu serbice' (free noodles) while a woman to my left belches and the old man on the right slurps down a bowl of noodles. Always amusing, this crowded lane of stainless steel counters never fails to yield a moment of truth: Koreans have an intensely personal and audible relationship with food. For a different kind of truth, I'm off to the brave new world of Apgujeong, the shopping and entertainment district for Seoul's A-list that's part commercial centre and part shrine to the Korean cult of beauty. After touring Seoul's heart of narcissism, I walk to Samwon Garden, a glorious barbecue restaurant to satisfy my urge to eat meat. Burn it off with a walk around the Seoul Tower and it's time to bathe. Bathhouses are everywhere, but I like Hurest Well Being in Myeong Dong because it's big and thinly attended in the afternoon. The euphoria that arises after an hour of rotating between hot and cold tubs is truly exhilarating. Back to the real world refreshed and thirsty, office workers and students have energised Myeong Dong's streets and alleys packed with teashops, restaurants and neon. Here I choose to initiate the all-important rehydration process at one of my favourite spots, a roadside plastic chair outside any convenience store. While replenishing vital fluids, a gaggle of curious university students approaches my table and shortly thereafter accepts an invitation to have a drink. The conviviality that builds over a bottle of *soju* (vodka-like spirit) is tempered momentarily by the realisation that the euphoria has dissipated. Not all is lost however, as I know I can do the whole thing again tomorrow.

The Perfect Day in
SHANGHAI

Best of Shanghai writer **Damian Harper** lives on the border of the French Concession in Shanghai.

A city that never sleeps would be taking it too far, but Shanghai sure wakes early. By 05.00 rubber-legged grannies are limbering up on the Bund with *taijiquan* forms and stretching exercises.

I'm not too far behind – my one-year-old daughter Emma wakes punctually at 06:00. On the metro by 07:00 with a copy of the Shanghai Daily and caffeine in the bloodstream, I'll be at the Bund within 30 minutes for a morning stroll. The Bund always rewards

exploration, especially in the early morning or as twilight turns to night. By 09:00 the city has climbed the gears and is firing on all cylinders. Crackling with commercial energy, Shanghai is most introspective in its parks and shrines. A visit to the Confucius Temple in the Old Town brings tranquillity and solitude, followed by *xiaolongbao* (steamed dumplings) at the Nanxiang Steamed Bun Restaurant in the (admittedly more frantic)

Yuyuan Bazaar. Recharged, I'll get a taxi to Renmin Square for an afternoon at the Shanghai Museum, and a swift visit to the Shanghai Art Museum if there's time. I'll reluctantly decline drinks at dusk on the Bund as I'd be retracing my steps, but dinner with friends at a French Concession restaurant is a must, sandwiched between drinks and chit-chat at neighbouring bars.

Parasols protect strollers on the Bund and echo the curves of Shanghai's Pearl Tower. **Greg Elms**

CITY HIGHLIGHTS

Temples of Angkor | Visit the wondrous temples – Angkor Wat, Ta Prohm and the Bayon.

Prek Toal | Wander through this sanctuary for some of the world's rarest water birds.

Old French Quarter | Trawl through the boutiques, galleries and restaurants of Psar Chaa and stop at Bar St...the name says it all.

Abacus | Dine at this excellent new restaurant, which serves wonderful French cuisine in a relaxed atmosphere.

Grand Hotel d'Angkor | Drop into cocktail happy hour at this classic colonial hotel for the perfect end to a day.

The Perfect Day in
SIEM REAP

Based in Phnom Penh, **Andrew Burke** is a journalist, photographer and author of *Laos*.

It doesn't matter how often I go to Siem Reap, I still get a buzz of anticipation when I know I'll be heading out to watch the sun rise over the temples of Angkor.

Sitting on the back of a *moto* in the half-light of pre-dawn, puttering along under the canopy formed by towering pillars of the forest and then turning left where the road ends at the enormous, mist-covered moat surrounding Angkor Wat is one of life's truly memorable journeys. Even more memorable, I've discovered over the years, is driving on past the hordes traipsing off their buses outside Angkor Wat and going straight to the Bayon. It's here, as you wander through the 216 enigmatic stone faces virtually alone, that you can't help but appreciate the history, the power, the ambition and the loss that Angkor represents. After this history feast, I like to head back to town for a bite of lunch at the Blue Pumpkin or one of the Khmer restaurants bordering the northeast side of Psar Chaa (Old Market). If it's hot I'll probably spend an extra hour getting an air-conditioned massage at Frangipani, before ducking back out to Angkor Wat or Preah Khan to take some afternoon photos. The evenings in Siem Reap are a testament to the power of the tourist dollar. When I first visited the town there were just two bars, but these days Bar St rocks pretty much all night and there's a good chance I'll be imbibing with friends in any number of establishments until the early hours. And after seeing the temples so many times, I don't have to get up too early in the morning.

The Perfect Day in
SINGAPORE

Melbourne-based travel writer **Paul Smitz** has written for numerous Lonely Planet guides.

A Singaporean day should start slowly, away from the crowds (plenty of time for those during the rest of the day), so I avoid anything even slightly resembling a shopping mall and take a long stroll along the quays.

I usually start at the jovial Alkaff Bridge near Robertson Quay and walk along the southern side of the Singapore River so that I can look across at the fetching pastels of Clarke Quay, eventually ending up in the foot traffic around Boat Quay. Next, I duck through the neoclassical columns of the Fullerton Hotel to have a lavish brunch within the hotel's magnificent European-style atrium (I booked a table several days ago to make

sure my stomach wouldn't be disappointed). Once this is digested, I walk across the river to Empress Place and refamiliarise myself with the wonderful galleries of the Asian Civilisations Museum, where I browse through illuminated Qurans, gorgeous textiles and other regional artefacts. If it's a clear-skied day, I'll take the subway to HarbourFront station and take a slow, scenic, late-afternoon ride on the high-altitude cable car that floats over Keppel Harbour to Sentosa Island and then does a loop via the splendid summit of Mt Faber. Next, it's a toss-up between a vegetarian snack (or three) in the exuberant sidestreets of Little India

or an early dinner in one of the fine French restaurants on Ann Siang Hill in Chinatown. But I'm liable just to make a beeline for the Newton Food Centre to the north of Orchard Rd and sit down at the stall selling delicious manta ray dishes. From here I'll take the night-safari tram ride through the superb Singapore Zoological Gardens. Now I'm ready for some drinking, which usually starts with a beer in one of the dramatic shophouse bars on Emerald Hill Rd, just off Orchard Rd, and ends with an early morning *shisha* (hooka-style pipe) on Arab St in Kampong Glam.

CITY HIGHLIGHTS

Hermitage | Lose yourself amid the treasures and interiors of one of the world's great art galleries.

Canal cruise | Hop on a water bus or river taxi for a boatman's perspective on the city's romantic architecture.

Mariinsky Theatre | Enjoy a world-class opera or ballet in the theatre that saw the premieres of the Nutcracker and Sleeping Beauty.

Petrodvorets | Admire the gilded Grand Cascade of 140 fountains at Peter the Great's palace by the Gulf of Finland.

Catherine Palace | Take in the gilded splendour of this opulent palace.

The Perfect Day in
ST PETERSBURG

Russia & Belarus author **Simon Richmond** first roamed goggle-eyed around St Petersburg in 1994.

St Petersburg is more of a late-to-bed than early-to-rise city.

So, although a dawn stroll along the Neva is a lovely idea, chances are I wouldn't be doing it unless I was in town during the White Nights of June and July when the sun barely sets and sleeping is practically out of the question. Let's start then with a leisurely post-breakfast mooch from Dvortsovaya pl (Palace Sq), along the Moyka river, past the riotously polychromatic Church of the Saviour on Spilled Blood and through the swirling iron gates of the Mikhailovsky Garden to the rear entrance of the Russian Museum for an essential fix of the masterworks of Russian art. After that I'd follow the Griboedov Canal, across Nevsky pr and past the wide open arms of Kazan Cathedral and the golden winged griffins of Bankovsky bridge, to lunch on excellent inexpensive Armenian food at Kilikia. From here it's a short walk to Sennaya Pl, the heart of 'Dostoevskyland', where the famed novelist lived and set Crime and Punishment. I'd soak up the still raffish atmosphere of the square, then take the metro to Staraya Derevnya in the city's north to tour the Hermitage's state-of-the-art storage facility displaying fascinating fragments from the museum's enormous collection: my favourite piece is the Ottoman ceremonial tent. Returning to the centre, I'd board a river boat for a relaxing late-afternoon tour along the canals. Later in the evening I'd head to the historic Mariinksy Theatre to attend an opera or ballet performance, dropping by Stolle on the way to snack on its sublimely delicious traditional Russian pies. After the show, if I was still hungry there's always the old standby of Café Idiot, or the more contemporary delights of Fasol. Finally I'd hit Datcha, one of the city's most happening DJ bars, for dancing and vodka toasts to the dawn of yet another glorious St Petersburg day.

the Perfect Day in
SYDNEY

Sally O'Brien is a *Sydney* and *New South Wales* guidebook author and on-off Sydney resident.

I swim a few dozen laps at the sparkling Andrew 'Boy' Charlton pool, when all the office workers are done and it's relatively quiet, and then, while enjoying the morning sun before it becomes too ferocious, I plot where to head for breakfast.

Fratelli Paradiso wins the call (as it almost always does), and so it's a tough walk up McElhone steps to Potts Point, which gets me sweating (and swearing) every time, but it's worth the effort. A flick through the Sydney Morning Herald brings me up to scratch on the latest political/business/entertainment (all three seem to merge in Sydney) scandals and then I'm off on a heritage binge, walking to delightful Elizabeth Bay House, then catching the Bondi Explorer to Vaucluse House where a sandwich lunch in the grounds is a picnic of sorts. Or maybe I want to spend the afternoon in the Art Gallery of NSW or the Museum of Contemporary Art (MCA), gazing at the latest blockbuster exhibitions. A sunset swim at Bronte or Tamarama beach puts me in the mood to see a few more bodies beautiful – so why not catch a brilliant Sydney Dance Company performance at the Sydney Opera House? Which hopefully is followed by cocktails and superb Asian cuisine at Longrain, and maybe a beer nightcap at the Hollywood Hotel.

HIGHLIGHTS

Island hiking | Traverse the rugged, lush and nearly untouched interiors of either island.

Snorkelling and diving | Sight rainbows of fish, and bigger animals like turtles, rays and sharks in the jaw-dropping reefs.

Whale watching | Spot the 'big fish' and dolphins from May to October.

Opunohu Valley | Experience a slice of Polynesian history and magical views in Mo'orea.

Pape'ete Market | Take a leisurely stroll through the vibrant show of fruit, shell and pareu vendors.

the Perfect Day in
TAHITI

The widely travelled **Celeste Brash** has lived in Tahiti since 2000 and is an author of *Tahiti*.

One of the treats of Tahiti and Mo'orea is the just-cool-enough-to-be-refreshing lagoon; when it's hot outside, a morning swim can be better than coffee for getting that energy pumping.

The islands wake up early and everyone heads to the market for fresh baguettes. I like to grab one for myself to dunk in a big cup of tea; I round off the meal with some bananas, grapefruit, mango or papaya. The Pape'ete Central Market is at its busiest in the mornings so it's a fun time to take a browse among the fruit, shell and pareu vendors – I always buy an ice-cold coconut at the entrance to sip on while I linger. Before the sun is too strong, I hop on the ferry to Mo'orea then take a trip up the Opunohu valley, through the archaeological sites and up to the viewpoint where basalt spires frame the famous Cook and Opunohu Bays below. Lunch at Hauru point or Cook's Bay is followed by some decadent lounging on the beach, a swim and a snorkel. For an extra special night out, the Beachcomber Hotel in Tahiti serves a buffet on Friday nights with some of the best traditional Tahitian food around and a spectacular Tahitian dance performance. Early nights are the norm on Tahiti but every now and then it's fun to go out on the town of Pape'ete to dance till dawn. The impressively varied club choices here range from teeny-bop hip hop to transvestite cabaret to local Tahitian bands, and even Latin music.

The Perfect Day in
TALLINN

Film critic, filmmaker, writer and photographer **Steve Kokker** has lived in Tallinn since 1996.

On my first day in Tallinn, I'd suggest being frighteningly responsible and waking up bright and early to head straight for the Old Town. It's better to have a wander before all the big tourist boats arrive.

Watch shop owners set up for their day, and step into a café on Raekoja plats for coffee and a light breakfast. Do your Upper and Lower Town sightseeing and picture-taking now. After a few hours, walk east along busy Narva maantee to get a flavour of Tallinn's relatively new downtown hustle and bustle; many of the buildings you see didn't exist even five years ago. Walk about 1.5km (1 mile) to the once-richest Tallinn suburb of Kadriorg until you get to the park of the same name. Check out Peter the Great's palace, then head out to Pirita. The 2km (1.2 miles) seaside road boasts vistas that are great any time of the day, but make a note to return here at sunset should you meet anyone appropriate for a romantic walk. Pirita beach awaits (or, if your wallet will let you, rent a yacht for a little tour of Tallinn Bay). With sand in each crevice of your body, it's time to cleanse – get the bus back to town and to the Kalamaja sauna. Sit and melt or get a vigorous rubdown, then, if energy allows, wander around Kalamaja for its great old wooden houses. It's a rough-edged part of town that no tourist usually sees but is worth a visit – the local dive bars serve up Tallinn's cheapest shots. After a power nap, head out to the once-again emptied Old Town for a night of eating, drinking and dancing.

The Perfect Day in
TIMBUKTU

Africa entices **Anthony Ham**, contributor to *Africa on a Shoestring*, into an extended yearly visit.

There's much to do in Timbuktu and little time to do it – from late morning until sunset the heat can be unbearable, even in winter, so I get up early when the sandy streets are still the colour of gold.

Picking up my daily bread from the roadside ovens of the Songhaï – it will be gritty with sand, like everything else in Timbuktu – I head for the Dyingerey Ber Mosque, one of West Africa's most evocative. While there I take a sneaky look to make sure that Timbuktu's famous door-that-cannot-be-opened (according to legend, if the door is opened evil will flood the world) hasn't come loose in the night, before heading for the roof and

fine morning views over the fabled city. As an act of still-early morning homage I doff my turban to the houses of the various explorers like Rene Caillié, Heinrich Barth and Gordon Laing, who made such a sacrifice to reach this faraway city. I'd also linger quietly by the well of Bouctou in the Ethnological Museum, and contemplate days of old when Tuareg nomads first camped here in the 11th century. Surrounded by the old town's crumbling mud houses, it can be almost impossible to imagine the city's days of legend. To get a clearer picture I make for the mud-and-wood tower of the appealing Sankoré Mosque, where 25,000 students once dignified

the halls. By now the sun is starting to drain colour from the day and energy from my legs, so I walk with ever-slowing steps to the Bar Restaurant Amanar where the desert blues music provides the perfect soundtrack to a slow Saharan afternoon. To make the most of the stunning desert light as sunset approaches, I hurry to the Hôtel Bouctou or the poignant Flamme de la Paix monument from where I leave the world behind for the solitude of the desert, either on foot to a neighbouring sand dune or by camel to an encampment of the Tuareg, a people with the most profound capacity for silence and campfire contemplation.

CITY HIGHLIGHTS

Tsukiji Market | Head over at the crack of dawn and watch frozen fish being flung about before sampling a fresh sushi breakfast.

Meiji-jing | Tokyo's most elegant Shint shrine, surrounded by a serene forest and impressive *torii* (temple gate).

Harajuku | Famous for its colourful pedestrian parade, out in full force on Sundays.

Roppongi Hills | Ultra-urbanity, squared. Spend an entire day here before a night out in Roppongi clubs.

Senso-ji | A living temple where the smells of incense and rice crackers mingle.

The Perfect Day in
TOKYO

Best of Tokyo author **Wendy Yanagihara** first toured the city on her mother's hip, aged two.

It's Sunday morning, and my circadian rhythms won't let me sleep in after an all-night tango in one of Roppongi's Latin-crazed dance clubs.

I take an iced coffee into Meiji-jing -neien, where, because it's June, the irises are in purply bloom and a bride and groom in layers of heavy kimono solemnly pose for photographs. After a walk in the shade and a stop at the shrine, I head outwards to Meiji-jing -bashi, where goth Lolitas are vamping for photographers, revelling in their alienation from the teeming Sunday crowds. Inspired by their style, I head into Shinjuku to hop on a train bound for Shimo-Kitazawa. The maze of little alleys spoking away from the train station are alive with tiny second-hand stores, artsy indie designers' shops and cool cafés. Laid-back hipsters with their inimitable Tokyo style browse the wares and socialise in the street. A handmade skirt of scrap fabric, a lacquer plate of cold *soba* and one used photography book later, I stumble upon a dark little café where a trio of twentysomethings is playing some mellow, Japanese-style samba. I linger over one more iced coffee, but it's getting late and I have a date with some friends. So I catch a train back into town, navigating crazy-hectic Shinjuku station, and surface at the east exit for the rendezvous.

We find each other and catch up on our latest adventures while walking to our favourite *izakaya* (bar or pub that serves food) nearby, with sunken tatami floors and excellent cheap eats. The beer gets flowing, the laughter gets going, and the kids at the next table have become our new best friends. Once we've had our fill of drink and merriment (and miso-basted mackerel), we're on the last train home and I'm ready for sweet sleep.

The Perfect Day in
TORONTO

Sarah Richards is a contributor to www.lonelyplanet.com.

I begin with a big breakfast and a bottomless cup of coffee at Fran's on College St, one of the city's most enduring 24-hour diners. Amid the bustle of early morning I watch heaving subway stations exhale long breaths of commuters and tourists, and inhale those stumbling home after a big night.

If it's sunny I'll meet up with friends and head to the Toronto Islands – a refuge of natural beauty miles away from the city's dominating skyline. If I tire of feeding the ducks and paddling around the pond in Centre Island Park I'll hop over to Algonquin Island and admire the laid-back artist colony. Wet days are best spent snaking through the bowels of PATH, a 30km (19mi) underground network of shops, atriums and food courts. For lunch I'll grab some friends to brave the Chinatown line-ups and we'll pile the communal round tables high with dishes. Afterwards I'll mosey on down to Queen St W and park myself at one of Lettieri's sidewalk tables to spend time sipping espresso and taking in the colourful show: a mixture of punks, goths and a smattering of skater types. With renewed energy I'll investigate Baldwin Village, where bohos mingle with the recent influx of martini-swilling urbanites. I love to dig deeper and find the odd Southeast Asian eatery.

The nearby Art Gallery of Toronto always beckons and, while I'm at it, I'll soak up old-fashioned splendour in the Grange, a Georgian manor complete with period furnishings and costumes. Dinner in Greektown is next and, with a mouth full of souvlaki, a swill of wine and a moment's contemplation, I could almost mistake the scene for the back streets of Thessaloniki. Finally, I'll cab back over to Little Italy to visit one (but probably more) of the bars along College St W. Even though I've spent the day in just one city, I'll feel like my soul has been fed an international diet of food, culture and good times.

The Perfect Day in
TRIPOLI

Syria & Lebanon author **Terry Carter** claims he'd fly to Lebanon for dinner if flights were cheaper.

I have to confess that my top day in Tripoli usually starts at Rafaat Hallab & Sons, the most famous maker of sweets in Tripoli and perhaps the Middle East.

Here I'll order up a plate of baklava with a pot of tea and eat myself silly. With the leftovers tucked away for later, I'll head to the souk to explore. My favourite part of the souk is exploring the disused *hammams* (baths) – the secret is knowing who has the keys to open them so you can check them out. Cafe Fahim is the next stop and while I love the interior, it's really about watching the old men play backgammon and smoke *sheesha* (water pipe). In the late afternoon I'll head to Al-Mina and go for a stroll and check out the shy couples (usually already married!) as they enjoy some time away from their families. If I'm up for a decent dinner, as opposed to a quick *shwarma* (kebab), I'll head to '46 for some great Italian fare. If it's winter and I'm heading to the Cedars the next day for some snowboarding, I'll call it a night, otherwise I'll check out the local kids flirting while smoking *sheesha* at one of the cafés on Rue Riad al-Solh.

CITY HIGHLIGHTS
Medieval souks | A shopper's delight.
Famous sweets | They're heaven-sent.
Citadel | Check out the excellent views of the city.
Hammams (baths) of the souq | Fascinating to explore.
Al-Mina | Take an afternoon walk along the waterfront.

Middle Eastern sweets filled with pistachio nuts for sale at a Tripoli market. **Bethune Carmichael**

CITY HIGHLIGHTS

Mole Antonelliana | Ride the panoramic lift which silently whisks you up to the roof terrace in just 59 seconds.

Caffè Torino | Sip a coffee under the porticos of Piazza San Carlo at this Turin institution.

Museo Egizio | Wonder at the fabulous collection of Egyptian artefacts, the largest outside Egypt.

Stratta | Sample a hazelnut chocolate at this historic shop on Piazza San Carlo.

Holy Shroud | Contemplate a copy of the Shroud at the Cathedral and learn more at the Museo della Sindone.

The Perfect Day in
TURIN

To the delight of *Italy* author **Josephine Quintero**, her daughter now lives in the country's north.

My day starts with a cappuccino kick-start at one of the sumptuous Baroque cafés, where I concentrate on ogling the cool-looking clientele rather than those fabulous ricotta-filled pastries; I want to strut, not waddle, to my next stop.

This, of course, being the designer boutiques of Via Roma. Next, it's time for an amble through old Turin and the cobbled streets that crisscross Via Guiseppe Garibaldi packed with intriguing shops, delis and antique stores. I duck into funky Caffè dei Guardinfanti on the corner of Mercanti and Barbaroux for my final pre-noon cappuccino – it's infra dig for Italians to drink cappuccino after midday.

Next I drop into Pizza Al Taglio on Via Tommaso for a slice (or two) of pizza, followed by a *gelataria* dessert from the handy ice-cream place right across the street. I'm munching on the move because I can't be in this part of town without ducking into the Palazzo Reale for its fabulous frescoes and tapestries. If I'm feeling holier-than-thou, the Cathedral's controversial Turin Shroud may beckon and, if I feel like an entertaining overdose of cheesy Shroud paraphernalia, I'll continue on to the Museo della Sindone. It's probably now *bicerìn* (coffee with chocolate) time, which can only mean Al Bicerìn on Piazza della Consolata; a

fabulous mirror-lined place that oozes 18th-century elegance. I'm still in time to watch the sun go down over the water, so I hightail it to the Piazza Vittorio and hop on one of the river's ferries. If I miss the boat, hey, that's no biggie; I'm in the right part of town to tweak my appetite (again) with some of the tasty pub-grub on offer. Then it's trattoria time, finishing up with a late-night visit to the bars and clubs that line the River Po.

CITY HIGHLIGHTS

City Palace | Towers, balconies and cupolas, oh my! Explore the palace complex and its vibrant museum.

Jagmandir Island | Snap lots of photos during the breezy boat ride to this photogenic palace-topped isle.

Bagore-ki-Haveli | Don't miss dazzling Rajasthani dance at this 18th-century *haveli* turned gallery and museum.

Eklingji | Explore this intriguing ancient temple complex and win friends in the small village behind it.

Vintage and Classic Car Collection | Marvel at the maharajas' 22 cars.

The Perfect Day in
UDAIPUR

Susan Derby co-wrote the *India* guide and rates India as one of her favourite places in the world.

My day begins with an *aloo paratha* and *chai masala* at the unfussy, lakefront Transmarine Restaurant.

The order takes time, so I scan a paper as bathers, laundry scrubbers and the occasional canine go about their morning rituals. Afterwards, I walk over the bridge and through the narrow streets of the old town, eventually making my way to Bansi Ghat for a one-hour boat trip to Jagmandir. The ride is half the fun. Having worked up an appetite, there's no choice but to grab a rickshaw and head for Natraj, a spot filled with locals and Gujarati tourists but few Westerners. For next to nothing, you get all the scrumptious Gujarati

thali you can handle. I digest while ambling through the refreshingly non-tourist-oriented streets in this section of the city, then rickshaw over to Battiyanni Chotta to browse the chock-a-block shops. I manage some good deals, if I do say so myself, on a miniature painting, handbag and a pair of glittery Rajasthani shoes that might just do the trick back home with a pair of worn jeans. Now it's time for a chill out and a break from the sun (an underused resource here, which a local group is aiming to change with future implementation of solar-powered rickshaws). I recline on the terrace of Lalghat Guesthouse,

catching a slight lakeshore breeze and some casual conversation. My evening holds a Rajasthani dance performance at Bagore-ki-Haveli; the dancers blow me away, and the puppeteer's clever antics are so amusing. Treating oneself to a fancy feast is a must, and the Udai Kothi rooftop is hard to pass up. After a fantastic dinner by candlelight, I dip my toes in the rooftop pool, cocktail in hand. Life in Udaipur is splendid from the top...but I look forward to life back down on earth, too.

The grand Udaipur City Palace cascades down the hillside to the shore of Lake Pachola. **Mark Andrew Kirby**

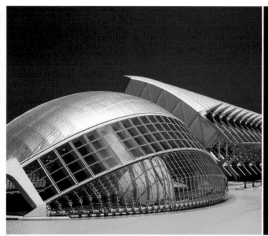

The Perfect Day in
VALENCIA

For nearly 20 years, **Miles Roddis** has lived in a shoebox-size apartment in Valencia's old quarter.

It's Sunday, earlyish, and for me the loveliest moment of the week. Most Valencianos are still in bed, many having turned in only a little before dawn.

I stroll across what's normally a densely trafficked boulevard, drop down to the old riverbed and jog upstream past weekend footballers limbering up, under Santiago Calatrava's stylishly curved bridge, beside formally landscaped gardens and more tousled areas. Before me looms the giant carapace of the Palau de les Arts, the latest and most gargantuan of the futuristic constructions within the City of Arts & Sciences. I run as far as its Oceanogràfic, Europe's largest aquarium, wondering if the darting fairy penguins are up and about yet. I do an about-turn, home and shower, then it's time for coffee, something sticky and the newspaper. I like a good view so I sit at a café terrace in Plaza de la Virgen, where the fountain spurts, dousing the magnificent representation of the River Turia, reclining like a Greek god. Museums and monuments are free on Sunday so I walk through the Barrio del Carmen – my favourite area for mooching, eating and late-night carousing – as far as the Instituto Valenciano de Arte Moderno (IVAM) to take in an exhibition. Lunch back home, then a restorative siesta (and let's demolish a stereotype: my indulgence isn't typical; very few Valencianos I know take a power nap, even in summer). One thing I do share with them, though, is a minor addiction to *horchata*, a sweet local drink made from pounded tiger nuts, so it's a short café stop to down a cold, refreshing glassful. I rest up until about 22:00, then meet friends in a bar on busy Calle Caballeros. A quick confab and we're off on tonight's route around the *barrio*: a *tapa* (small portion) of *boquerones* (anchovies in vinegar) here, a beer there, a *ración* (bigger than a *tapa*; I'm getting peckish) of *chipirones* (baby squid) in a third bar, and so on until sleepiness and the thought of Monday morning drive me home.

Valencia's wonderful City of Arts and Sciences houses museums, an oceanarium and an arts centre. **Neil Setchfield**

The Perfect Day in
VANCOUVER

John Lee lives in downtown Vancouver with a view of snowcapped mountains from his window.

Any hike around the sights and attractions of Western Canada's leading city should start with a stomach-bulging big breakfast, so I head straight for Sophie's Cosmic Cafe, a Kitsilano diner legend that's stuffed with old-school music and movie memorabilia.

I unfold a map over my eggs Benedict and plot my ride to the University of BC. It would be easy to spend a day at the campus – the naturist Wreck Beach maybe – but instead I'm heading for the Museum of Anthropology. When I arrive, I quickly understand why this is perhaps the city's best cultural attraction. The Haida artworks are fascinating, but it's the forest of totem poles,

dramatically set against a glass atrium overlooking the water, that blow most visitors away. I hop back on the bus towards Granville Island, nestled beneath a classic ironwork bridge. I spend some time ducking into the glass, jewellery and furniture artisan studios dotting this former industrial area: it's now the city's leading tourist hang-out. An organic coffee from the bustling public market restores my flagging energy before I board one of the cute, bathtub-sized ferries for a quick skim across False Creek. Walking up the stiff incline of Hornby St, I stroll to Gastown, the city's oldest neighbourhood. I spend some time here browsing through galleries and

shops before continuing to Chinatown. With its streets of traditional apothecaries, grocery stores hawking unfamiliar fruits and the occasional bucket of live toads, this is Vancouver's liveliest neighbourhood. For a calming respite, I head across to the Dr Sun-Yat Sen Classical Chinese Garden. As I watch the turtles sunning themselves around the pond, I plan my evening. The Railway Club, at the corner of Dunsmuir St and Seymour St, is my favourite of the city's bars. With the ambience of a grungy British pub and a beer selection that always includes a few lip-smacking regional brews, there's a nightly roster of eclectic live music with plenty of local bands.

Enjoy a coffee and the view of Vancouver's skyline from Granville Island. **Chris Cheadle**

The Perfect Day in
VENICE

Visiting Italy on her honeymoon ignited **Laetitia Clapton**'s love affair with the country.

The day begins with obligatory coffee and croissants on Campo Santa Maria Formosa.

I give myself time to digest while watching the comings-and-goings on the square. Fed and watered, I wander over in the direction of Rialto, stopping at the Fondaco dei Tedeschi to remind myself that even a Post Office in Venice is palatial. Ignoring the uninspiring shops on Rialto Bridge I walk up the outside steps, pausing to watch the traffic on the Grand Canal, and over into Rialto Market. Even if I'm not buying, the fresh produce stalls and the splendid fish market are an insight into the Venetian way of life – watching customers lug heavy bags I wonder if they ever wish the city had room for cars. On my way through San Polo I potter around the shops, eschewing the questionable Murano glass fish-in-bowls for a bargain pair of fishnet tights or a beaded necklace. My stomach's now rumbling and the elaborately decorated Caffè Frari is perfect for a *panini* (sandwich) and a flick through the paper. Refuelled, I pop into Venice's largest church, the Franciscan Chiesa di Santa Maria Gloriosa dei Frari then get my Tintoretto fix from the Scuola Grande di San Rocco. All that culture's made me thirsty and my watch is chiming 'spritz o'clock' (Italian white wine and soda with Campari or Aperol), so I head to Campo Santa Margarita for a glass of the Venetian aperitif with Aperol (Campari is too bitter for my sweet tooth). Kids play football, young Venetian studs check out glamorous-looking girls and families meet up on this lively square. Dinner is a real treat and I head over to Giudecca and Cip's, the Hotel Cipriani's less formal restaurant. As I sup on beautiful sea-bream and admire the view of St. Mark's and Dorsoduro I wonder if there's really any other way to live. Later the gleaming hotel boat chauffeurs me back to my Venetian home, sated and content.

Gondolas await tourists and lovers on Venice's romantic waterways. **Juliet Coombe**

The Perfect Day in
VIENNA

When not on the road, **Neal Bedford** spends much of his time on the balcony of his Vienna flat.

It's hard for me to choose a top day in my city of choice, but as I write this in the heat of summer, the following would satisfy my current urban needs.

I kick-start my day with a paprika and tomato omelette at Kent, the best Turkish restaurant this side of Istanbul. Once this has settled nicely in my stomach, I wander the Brunnenmarkt searching for fresh fruit and vegetables to accompany me on my day's outing. A quick ride on the J tram down to the Museums Quartier (MQ) follows, where I make a beeline for the Leopold Museum and spend far too long gazing in awe at Schiele's work. Back in the expanse of the MQ, a bit of sun and a milky coffee are perfect refreshments. My feet then lead me across the Ringstrasse and into the Innere Stadt via the Hofburg and the National Bibliothek's glorious Prunksaal. Once my system is overloaded with baroque splendour, I make a few quick phone calls to determine who's up for lunch and a beer at the Kleines Café. As the afternoon heat scorches the city, I make a beeline for the Alte Donau for a long, lazy swim before crossing town to my apartment, where I spruce myself up for the evening's festivities. If the weather is still holding, it's back to the MQ to enjoy the last of the day's heat and the circus of tourists and locals parading up and down the square's long thoroughfare. Once the entertainment has subsided, it's homeward bound, only to be ship-wrecked at Rhiz, my local and, unsurprisingly, favourite bar in town. The hours slip away until I realise it's well past the witching hour and the lure of my bed is too strong to ignore.

The Perfect Day in
WASHINGTON DC

Californian **Ryan Ver Berkmoes'** long writing career has included more than 10 Lonely Planet books.

For me a visit to DC almost always starts and ends on the Mall. It's all here really and first-time visitors are regularly blown away when all its iconic places, that are almost clichés, are seen up close.

The Capitol is a magnificent building; notice the play of light on the columns. Heading west past the parade of Smithsonians, I'd be sure to stop in at the East Building of the National Gallery (IM Pei's masterpiece is still fresh three decades later; there's a great café on the skylit lower level). Then I'd visit the National Air and Space Museum (Apollo 11, need I say more) followed by the National Museum of American History (sort of like the nation's attic of treasures). Next it's a visit to the Washington Monument, which looks bigger in person. I'd spare a glance for the fortified White House to the north and if the president is flying overhead in his helicopter (a frequent occurrence) I'd show him a finger (two over from the thumb) to express my feelings for his administration. The huge new World War II memorial stands at the entrance to the reflecting pools; sadly it's a miscue and doesn't even begin to capture the event. Circling north, I'd pause at what is possibly the most eloquent war commemoration anywhere, the Vietnam Veterans Memorial. After this sombre pause, I'd head to the Lincoln Memorial to uplift my spirits by reading the words of this most humane and visionary of leaders. By now I'm ready for a cocktail. If the weather allows, one of the many outdoor cafés in Dupont Circle (17th St NW rarely disappoints) will fit the bill nicely. Suitably refreshed, I'd stroll about looking for a restaurant from the neighbourhood's countless choices. A nightcap amid the woody and eclectic charms of the Tabard Inn is the perfect way to end the day.

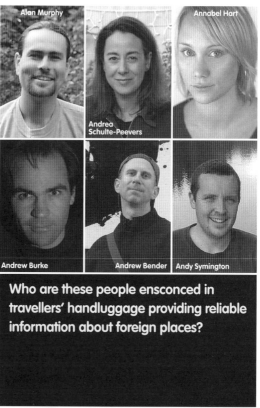

Alan Murphy

Andrea Schulte-Peevers

Annabel Hart

Andrew Burke

Andrew Bender

Andy Symington

Who are these people ensconced in travellers' handluggage providing reliable information about foreign places?

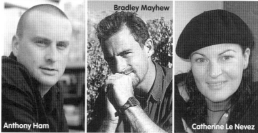

Anthony Ham

Bradley Mayhew

Catherine Le Nevez

Celeste Brash

Conner Gorry

Damian Harper

Daniel Schechter

David Atkinson

Etain O'Carroll

Gemma Pitcher

George Dunford

Jenny Walker

Joe Bindloss

Lonely Planet authors are like the little person who operates the light in the fridge: dependable and a crucial guide to illuminating what's there. They're a diverse bunch of freelancers united by a passion for travel, questioning minds and the chutzpah to find the answers. And they can write to boot.

Joe Cummings

John A Vlahides

John Lee

John Spelman

The average LP author generally possesses a range of qualifications. There's the formal educative certification, but also a healthy number of life experiences that make them experts in judging a comfortable bed, a superior wonton soup or a scam when they see one. An example author may use their hard-earned philosophy degree to spend a year as a peripatetic croissant-maker, teacher and dog-handler in a number of countries and states where they're speaking a second (sometimes fifth or sixth) language. All the while, writing and photographing their surrounds.

Neil Wilson

Nick Ray

Patrick Witton

Paula Hardy

Paul Smitz

Ray Bartlett

Regis St Louis

Richard Watkins

Robert Kelly

When they're not working for LP, authors work as academics, with NGOs, as writers of fiction and features, lawyers, translators, bloggers and broadcasters. Along the way they've worked as shop assistants, in bars, as editors and deckhands.

Whether at work or at rest, authors' inquisitive minds lead them to a thoughtful engagement with everyday life: be it in their hometown, or in a foreign place. It's in this spirit that LP authors have eaten snails and entrails, swum with giant rays, drunk in an outback pub or spent weeks without electricity and hot water.

Robert Landon

Robert Reid

Rob Whyte

Ryan Ver Berkmoes

When in Rome they sip espresso; when in Sweden they roll in the snow after a sauna; in New Zealand they bungy; in Beirut they take sheesha…

Most obviously, Lonely Planet authors are people. They all have families and friends, and belong to and visit communities for which they care for enormously. They're also hyper aware of their community of readers who choose an LP author as a travelling companion. LP authors have an unswerving respect for and dedication to their readers. It's to this end: they give you their favourite days.

Sally O'Brien

Sandra Bao

Sara Sam Benson

Simon Richmond

Sarina Singh

Simon Sellars

Steve Fallon

Steve Kokker

Steven Martin

Susan Derby

Terry Carter

Verity Campbell

Wendy Yanagihara

Index

A
Australia
Brisbane 19
Melbourne 61
Sydney 90
Austria
Vienna 102

B
Belgium
Brussels 20
Bolivia
La Paz 51
Brazil
Rio de Janeiro 80

C
Cambodia
Phnom Penh 73
Siem Reap 87
Canada
Montreal 65
Toronto 95
Vancouver 100
China
Beijing 11
Hong Kong 41
Shanghai 86
Colombia
Bogotá 16
Cuba
Havana 38
Czech Republic
Prague 77

E
Egypt
Cairo 23
England
Bath 10
Brighton 18
London 55
Manchester 59
Estonia
Tallinn 92

F
Finland
Helsinki 39
France
Paris 71

G
Germany
Berlin 14
Munich 67

H
Hungary
Budapest 21

I
India
Delhi 29
Jaisalmer 44
Mumbai 66v
Udaipur 98
Indonesia
Bali 6
Ireland
Cork 27
Galway 35
Kilkenny 48
Israel
Jerusalem 45
Italy
Florence 34
Milan 64
Turin 97
Venice 101

J
Japan
Tokyo 94

L
Laos
Luang Prabang 57
Lebanon
Beirut 12
Tripoli 96

M
Malaysia
Kuala Lumpur 50
Mali
Bamako 7
Djenné 30
Timbuktu 93
Mexico
Cabo San Lucas 22
Mexico City 62
Puerto Vallarta 78
Morocco
Essaouira 33
Marrakesh 60

N
Nepal
Kathmandu 47
Pokhara 75
New Zealand
Auckland 5
Queenstown 79
Rotorua 81
Northern Ireland
Belfast 13

P
Panama
Bocas del Toro 15
Panama City 70
Peru
Lima 53
Poland
Krakow 49
Portugal
Lisbon 54

R
Russia
St Petersburg 89

S
Scotland
Edinburgh 32
Glasgow 36

Singapore 88
South Africa
Cape Town 24
Johannesburg 46
South Korea
Seoul 85
Spain
Barcelona 9
Madrid 58
Valencia 99
Sultanate of Oman
Muscat 68

T
Tahiti 91
Thailand
Bangkok 8
Chiang Mai 25
Phuket 74
Turkey
Istanbul 43

U
United Arab Emirates
Abu Dhabi 4
Dubai 31
USA
Boston 17
Chicago 26
Dallas 28
Honolulu &
Waikiki 42
Las Vegas 52
Los Angeles 56
Miami 63
New York City 69
Philadelphia 72
Portland 76
San Diego 82
San Francisco 83
Seattle 84
Washington DC 103

V
Vietnam
Hanoi 37
Ho Chi Minh City 40

THE PERFECT THREESOME. YOU, US AND THE CITY.

THE CITIES BOOK

Lonely Planet's follow-up to the best-selling *The Travel Book* is a full-color pictorial celebrating the microcosms of human achievement that are cities. Taking our cue from the buzz on the street, *The Cities Book* captures the individual flavor of each city through the eyes of the typical citizen: in dazzling, edgy images, hot conversation topics, urban myths, the best places to eat, drink and to seek out after dark.

CITY GUIDE

City Guides are the perfect companion for exploring a city. Written by experienced authors who know the town intimately, city guides are smart and streetwise and are your way in to the heart of a city.

The Citiescape series – Asia

If you liked *The Cities Book* you'll love these cute and stylish little gift books, each of which focuses on an iconic Asian city. Each book looks at the individual personality of that city and explores the way in which its character has evolved and how it is expressed in the daily life of the city, whether that be the feisty, energetic hedonist that is Bangkok, or the dynamism of whizz-kid Tokyo. The books combine a mix of candid and beautiful photographs with unique and insightful facts and commentary about the city.

Available individually, all ten titles also stack up very smartly together into a cube that no coffee table should be seen without.

BEST OF

Best Of guides are the ultimate pocket guide for short-trip visitors, highlighting the best a city has to offer. Features include insider tips from expert authors, and information on not-too-miss restaurants, bars, clubs and hotels.

Individual New Titles

Bangkok
Beijing
Delhi
Ho Cho Minh City
Hong Kong
Kathmandu
Mumbai
Singapore
Sydney
Tokyo

THIS IS NOT
THE END

www.lonelyplanet.com